W9-AQN-862

POWER AND PROPERTY IN INCA PERU

BY SALLY FALK MOORE

COLUMBIA UNIVERSITY PRESS

MORNINGSIDE HEIGHTS, NEW YORK, 1958

84206

COPYRIGHT © 1958 COLUMBIA UNIVERSITY PRESS, NEW YORK
PUBLISHED IN GREAT BRITAIN, CANADA, INDIA, AND PAKISTAN
BY THE OXFORD UNIVERSITY PRESS
LONDON, TORONTO, BOMBAY, AND KARACHI
Library of Congress Catalog Card Number: 58:12215
MANUFACTURED IN THE UNITED STATES OF AMERICA

POWER AND PROPERTY
IN INCA PERU

FOR CRES

This study, prepared under the Graduate Faculties of Columbia University, was selected by a committee of those Faculties to receive one of the Clarke F. Ansley awards given annually by Columbia University Press.

• PREFACE

In writing a book on one aspect of a culture it is difficult to proceed without presuming that the reader knows the
background. This is an entirely unreasonable, but necessary,
assumption. Otherwise the book must repeat at length what
is amply discussed elsewhere. Though I have not left the reader
utterly to his recollection of Inca culture, the Introduction includes only the briefest of general descriptions.

Those who would like more background material on the Inca
are referred to the account by John Howland Rowe in the
Handbook of South American Indians. It is by far the best
modern summary of Inca culture. While not comparable to
Rowe as a reference work, Prescott's classic *History of the Conquest of Peru* has the advantages of readability and accessi-
bility. There are such a number of other general books on the
Andes and the Inca that they cannot be discussed critically
here. Suffice it to say that few are wholly satisfactory.

As for works on Inca law, three contemporary writers ought
to be mentioned: Hermann Trimborn, Jorge Basadre and
Horacio Urteaga. Urteaga's "La organización judicial en el imperio de los Incas" is a very brief, barely annotated and wholly
conventional summary. Jorge Basadre has written a much more
extensive book, the first volume of a series, entitled *Historia del
derecho peruano*. Basadre's book, though it contains good material, is somewhat inconclusive and diffuse, and relies very
heavily on secondary sources. He is discursive and given to
debating such questions as whether the Inca ruler was a despot
or a tyrant. Hermann Trimborn is well-known to anyone interested in the Inca. He is a careful scholar who over a period
of many years has produced numerous well-annotated articles

on the Inca, some of them particularly concerned with Inca law. Even if one finds his Kulturkreis framework unpalatable and disagrees with other aspects of his approach, one cannot but be in his debt.

Thanks are also due to a number of other people. I am particularly grateful to three scholars who had no direct connection with this book, but who have had much to do with forming my attitude toward its subject. I owe thanks to law Professor K. N. Llewellyn whose lively interest in anthropology was contagious, to anthropology Professor A. L. Kroeber whose interest in law gave me much encouragement, and to the late Harry Tschopik, to whom I owe my introduction to Inca culture.

I would like to thank Professors W. D. Strong, who was Chairman of the Committee sponsoring this work as a Ph.D. dissertation, and Charles Wagley, a member of the Committee. Both were a source of excellent suggestions and ready encouragement. Their interest in Peru, in the Americas, and in the unorthodox, made it a pleasure to work with them. To my colleague Robert Stigler, also a member of the Committee, my appreciation for interest and friendship through the years.

Last and largest is Columbia University, to which I owe my formal education, a handful of degrees, and the Ansley Award which makes possible the present publication. It is difficult to thank a University, but one cannot thank it enough.

SALLY FALK MOORE

September, 1958

• CONTENTS

POWER AND PROPERTY
IN INCA PERU

• INTRODUCTION

The Inca [1] were a Quechua speaking people of the Cuzco region of Peru. In less than a century before the Spaniards' arrival in 1532 the Inca had subjugated the area between Ecuador and Chile. Illiterate, but highly organized, they incorporated conquered tribes and valley-states into their governmental system, imposing their emperor, their governors, their national religion, language, and taxes on the diverse defeated peoples. Much of the information left to us refers to the Inca culture alone. This gives an appearance of unity and uniformity to an empire which had much regional variation. The population of the area in 1532 has been estimated as anywhere from 4,500,000 to 7,500,000. [2]

How was it possible for five million or more relatively primitive people to be organized under one ruler? How were they taxed, how were they governed? These are questions which have been asked since the 16th century and have more often than not, been answered with extreme naïveté. From descriptions which attribute the nature of the Inca empire solely to the wise legislation of the Inca emperors, to those which attribute it to the vigorous traditions of the communally-owned peasant villages, there has been much left out.

The questions about Inca government are worth asking again. The study of political organization has unfortunately urgent reasons. A knowledge of the law and government of primitive peoples may add usefully to what is known of the range and dynamics of man's political behavior. The Inca empire as an early form of the state, suggests many things about its gigantic relative, the modern state. The same focal points can be used for the political study of a primitive as a complex society: the nature of the elite, the relations between governing and governed, the right to use force, the connection between power and the economic order, the equilibrium of the political structure, the rationale of the system, etc.

The Inca display a range of paradoxical characteristics worthy of any state today. The highest nobility was by its own criminal standards morally self-indulgent, yet figuratively and literally holier-than-thou, since it claimed divine ancestry. Though there was ostensibly neither poverty nor crime in the empire, provision was made to cope with both. Power, supposedly held only by the most meritorious, was generally inheritable. These are but a few of the lot. Inca culture, in short, was carried by a human society, and can thus be expected to have had a great tower of vanity and rationalization constructed on its base of real achievements and real failures. What we know of the Inca is a mélange of what they thought of themselves, what the Spanish conquerors heard, saw, believed or thought it useful to say.

This book was written to wring out of the sources whatever they would yield of precise information on law and government. In emphasizing the active and functioning side of social organization, rather than the purely structural, inquiries about law and government require practical answers to practical questions.

Since the Inca economy was based on intensive agriculture, the principal wealth was in land and land produce. Hence, to inquire into land law is to start at the base of the power structure and see who had a right to what. In the taxation system, the government is seen hard at work keeping itself going. Tax law tells much about the nature of government, the price it exacted and the price it had to pay for self-maintenance. In the law of inheritance is imbedded the tendency of the class structure to perpetuate itself, and the privileges and obligations that went with it. Through the criminal law there is to be had a glimpse into Inca ethics. What conduct was more reprehensible and what was less so? From whom was morality required and from whom was it not?

Many popular preconceptions totter in the face of the legal material. But more important than destroying foolish theories, which can be found and destroyed about anything, the legal material adds substantially to the reconstructed picture of the Inca empire and culture.

Inca civilization was undoubtedly one of the most developed in the Americas. Its signal achievement is usually regarded as that of political organization. Writing was unknown to the Inca; they probably did not have a recorded calendar, and among their technical resources there was neither the wheel nor the smelting of iron. They used knotted cords (*quipus*) to record numerical information and as mnemonic devices.

The Inca had mastered the techniques of irrigation, terracing, fertilizers and crop rotation. Maize, squash, beans, potatoes and a host of other vegetables were the staple crops. Many fruits were grown. Food was stored and preserved on a large scale by drying and by freezing. Llamas, the principal domesticated animals, were used as beasts of burden as well as for their wool and meat.

Large scale buildings, temples, palaces and fortresses of stone were constructed by the Inca, who were also prodigious weavers of fine cloth, and skilled metallurgists who used copper, silver, gold, tin, mercury and arsenic. Elaborate irrigation works and water-piping systems were built by the Inca, and many rivers were canalized.

There were some planned towns and some large population centers in the empire. Cuzco, the capital city, has been said to have had a population of 100,000 taxpayers. Yet Cuzco was not an urban center in the European sense. It was a ceremonial center surrounded by a ring of small villages, each with its own fields. The extensive empire was linked together by a network of roads, the two most important running the length of the coast and the highlands. The central government re-

quired the maintenance of a system of post runners to permit
rapid communication at great distances.

What is most interesting about all of the basic techniques
used by the Inca is that the archeological record shows that
the techniques were all known and used in the Central Andean
area for about a thousand years before the Spanish Conquest.
The Inca domination of the area dated only from about a century before the Conquest. While basic technological advances
had been slight for a thousand years, there were considerable
social and political developments. Political units steadily increased in size and there was an expansion of the application
of techniques such as irrigation. Population increased. The
economic surplus increased. The development culminated in
the Inca empire.

There is no doubt that Inca culture was highly developed,
both technologically and socially. However, the Inca governmental system has often been idealized out of all proportion.
It is a failing well-known among anthropologists that one may
have an exaggerated affection for whatever people one special-
izes in. The Inca have been too much loved. No society of
ants or bees runs more smoothly than the political system
usually attributed to the Inca. Lauded for great military and
administrative skill, and praised as social planners, the Inca
have come to occupy an all too sacred and superhuman position in the literature.

Has there ever been a government worthy of the heavy-
breathing eulogies unhesitatingly heaped on the Inca?

To conclude . . . however stern the Incaic rule may have been,
it was never unjust; however much the greatness and splendor of
the highly placed may have been served and enhanced, the well-
being of the humble was never lost to sight; however much may
have been demanded of the people in the way of personal labor and
of tribute, society as a whole was well compensated by the measure
of peace and security, of plenty and of leisure, that was assured to
it by the Incaic rule.[3]

It is all very well to praise the Inca, who were surely a remarkable people, but it is not quite so worthy to praise them for what they did not do. Deplorable instances of excessive adulation abound. For example, consider two effusive social reformers of the 1920s, one in France,[4] the other in Bolivia,[5] calling loudly for the remodeling of their countries along the lines of an Inca utopia. Ideas about Inca government and law have been mistaken for descriptions of Inca government and law. Strong feelings about the matter have tended to cause the same generalizations to be repeated interminably, with little or no regard for the evidence which might settle some of the controversies.

It is not with any wish to disparage Inca political achievements that this book has been written, but rather to undo somewhat the utopian idealization, and present instead a more plausible and, to my view, more realistic picture.

Such responsible modern scholars as Louis Baudin and Hermann Trimborn have emerged with contrasting conceptions of the Inca economic and political system. Baudin entitled his famous book *L'Empire socialiste des Inka,* while Trimborn speaks of the "estado feudal incaico." [6] Trimborn's emphasis on the exploitative role of the Inca upper classes has offended the sensibilities of Luís Valcárcel. Among many other works, Valcárcel has recently produced one of the most extensive descriptions of Inca culture to emerge from Peru.[7] In his patriotic account, Inca Peru was all collective property and all on a high moral plane. Valcárcel's admiration for the Inca welfare state makes him impatient with European writers. He complains that they have a permanent prejudice against the idea that native peoples might have an "alta concepción de la vida." While Valcárcel is heard all the way from Peru saying "socialism," Karl Wittfogel murmurs in an unmurmurable aside, "the Inca empire represents a simple pattern of hydraulic property and society." [8] In his Chicago University dissertation

John Murra convincingly shows the evidence for the welfare state to have been "sketchy and indefinite." [9] Rowe says the Inca government was "an unqualified despotism" and returns the question of Inca socialism to the reader by saying that whether the Inca were socialist or not depends on one's definition of socialism.[10] Great interest and much confusion have resulted from the use of Inca government to illustrate political theories. To give the full taste of the social sauce, one can enjoy such mixtures as Murdock's:

Socialism, linked with democracy in Marxian theory, was consistent in Peru with monarchy and aristocracy. The Inca system exerted a leveling influence, creating a uniform standard of living throughout the empire. If it thus realized the ideal of equality, it was equality only within a given social class.[11]

The sort of theorizing which brings Murdock to imply that equality within a social class was an achievement of Inca socialism hardly clarifies one's picture of Inca culture. The Procrustean bed of political theory, particularly utopian political theory, is a bad place to put to rest such assorted information as we have about the Inca.

Ultimately all knowledge of the Inca empire derives from a rather ambiguous lot of 16th and 17th century manuscripts. As a consequence of inconsistency, plagiarism, and incompleteness in these documents, many liberties can be taken in describing the Inca culture. Evidence can be found to support precisely opposite theories. It is a case in which the scholar can be all too much master of his material.

Many of the chroniclers were priests, while some were soldiers, and there were a few administrators and judges. In addition to these accounts there are innumerable native and Spanish answers to questionnaires about the Inca issued at various times in the 16th century by the Spanish kings. The modern published versions of the 16th and 17th century manuscripts, rather than the originals, have been used in the preparation of this book.

Of great assistance through the maze of sources are the modern bibliographical works of Philip A. Means,[12] and the remarks on sources of Baudin [13] and Rowe.[14] Of these, Rowe's comments can be applauded without reservation, while the others are better used for biographical and bibliographical information than for evaluation. Rowe's bibliography, itself, is extremely useful.

The greatest of the chroniclers and the one on whom I relied most heavily was Father Bernabé de Cobo, a Jesuit. His *Historia del Nuevo Mundo* is still one of the most comprehensive and level-headed accounts of the Inca. However, this great work was completed in 1653, more than a hundred years after the Spaniards' fateful landing at Tumbez. Though Cobo was careful and wise in using earlier documents, one cannot help but regret that his was not a first-hand investigation of the Inca at the time of the Conquest, but a historical study written a century later.

Of the soldier-chroniclers, the most distinguished writer was Cieza de León, whose *Crónica del Perú* has the advantage of having been written from immediate experience. Cieza was in a particularly good position to make valuable observations since he was in Peru from 1534 to 1551; he traveled widely during that time, and kept journals of what he saw.

In the search for material on government and law some fragments are to be found in almost all the chronicles. But there is a concentration of information in certain works. Apart from Cobo and Cieza de León, one of the most useful writers is the Licenciado Polo de Ondegardo on whom Cobo relied quite heavily. A highly educated man, a judge, an administrator and a soldier, Polo had a considerable interest in and knowledge of things Incaic. Another judge and government official whose work is of particular present interest was Licenciado Fernando de Santillán, who wrote a "Relación" answering questions about Inca institutions posed by Prince Philip in 1553, and making recommendations as to how the Spanish should proceed in dealing with Peru. Both Polo and Santillán held the position of *Oidor* of the Royal Audiencia of Lima. A third jurist of the same period was the Licenciado Francisco Falcón, who gives some useful information on the Inca in the course of protesting Spanish injustices to the natives. All three of these men deplored Spanish abuses and advocated some measure of return to Inca custom in tax matters. Happily for us, they did describe the taxation system and give much information on Inca administration.

Another "Relación" of particular interest to this study has been that of Cristóbal de Castro and Diego de Ortega Morejón written in 1558. Because it describes a single valley, rather than the whole empire, it has the advantage of particularity. The Chincha Valley was a large and powerful one before the Inca conquest. It had been under Inca rule for at least forty years [15] and probably more by the time the Spaniards arrived in Peru. This would seem to have been time enough for sufficient integration into the Inca Empire to be a good example of the extent to which conquered areas were assimilated. Castro and Ortega Morejón based their account on the testimony of elderly officials of the Chincha Valley, and give much material relevant to a study of government.

Garcilaso de la Vega is perhaps the most widely known of the chroniclers. We owe a great deal of the idealization of the Inca to him. The son of one of the first Spanish conquerors and his mistress, a woman of royal Inca lineage, Garcilaso's principal claim to authoritativeness is biological, rather than scholarly. Born in Peru in 1539, he went to Spain in 1561. Some forty, or more years later, he started work on his *Comentarios reales,* a long eulogy of Inca culture and people, here and there sprinkled with information. He garnered his facts from some of the other chroniclers of the day, principally Blas Valera, but partly from his own creative memory. As far as Garcilaso was concerned an Inca could do no wrong.

Unfortunately Garcilaso has been very widely read and

overrated. This is in part because of his consistent praise of the Inca. The Spanish conquerors mercilessly exploited the Indians economically, decapitated (literally and figuratively) their government, and tried to destroy their religion. In an effort to rationalize this devastation some chroniclers fell back on the evils of idolatry, grew indignant over purported Inca tyranny, and showed a general contempt for the Inca way of life, and for the Indians themselves. Some of the chroniclers such as the intelligent judge, Polo de Ondegardo, wrote their works largely to protest the Spanish methods and attitudes. But many of the writings of the day—and surely most of those written to please the Spanish administrators of the Crown—were attempts to justify the Spanish position. This can be said of much that was written by and at the behest of the famous Viceroy Toledo, who came to Peru in 1569 and dominated that country until 1582 when he returned to Spain.[16]

In contrast was the work of Garcilaso, who had only lauda- tory things to say of his ancestors. Philip Ainsworth Means classified the two attitudes: the pro-Inca as "Garcilassan," the pro-Spanish as "Toledan," and listed all the chroniclers he could classify under one or the other.[17] Means' enthusiasm for Inca culture led him to hate Toledo as a symbol of 16th-cen- tury Spanish interests, and to heap praise on Garcilaso as the champion of the unappreciated Inca. His choice of champion was unfortunate, since Garcilaso was somewhat too inventive a writer.

On the other side, prejudice in favor of the "Toledan" pre- conceptions also qualifies the use that can be made of the an- swers to the questionnaires issued by the Spanish.[18] On the surface the questionnaires appear to have been put forth out of a genuine curiosity about native institutions. But they were at least partly designed to elicit answers that would justify and support the Spanish position. The Indians were generally il- literate; the questioning and recording of answers was done by Spaniards. The answers were sometimes in the form of prepared statements which were read to a group of distinguished octogenarian Indians, many of them former officials, who then affirmed that what had been read to them was correct.[19] To what extent the answers were those of the Indians, and to what extent the version of the investigator and recorder cannot be exactly determined. There is no doubt from the precisely repeated wording of many answers by different Indians that the hand of the scribe was strong in forming the text.

Without discussing particular sources any further,[20] suffice it to say that the material available is tantalizingly incomplete. Whole parts of manuscripts are lost. When information is given it is often in the most general terms, and the details are generally missing or fragmentary. As a general criterion for documentary evaluation, where practical I have given greater credence to specific remarks than to generalizations. To make sense of the generalizations once confronted with contradictory details is not too difficult if one bears in mind that the Inca emperors and nobles seem to have thought of themselves as designing a form of government.

It is their idealized plan which is generally described as the Inca practice. But the very chroniclers who reiterate the utopian symmetry of the plan give many other details which show how much more there was to the story. It is the purpose of this study to examine the Inca legal and political system in practice rather than in plan.

Unfortunately the tendency to repeat the chroniclers' generalizations rather than reinvestigate the nature of Inca government has been quite common. As Rowe has said in his on-the-whole excellent summary in the *Handbook of South American Indians*,[21] anyone wishing detailed information must go back to the chroniclers themselves, as the secondary materials are not adequate. Rowe's article itself is too short to go beneath the general outlines of the Inca government plan to examine and discuss the more controversial aspects of Inca practice. The meandering and inconsistent quality of the sources on the Inca permit opposite arguments to be made on the basis of the same texts. In this book a picture of Inca government and law has been reconstructed which differs in significant respects from the traditional conception. Yet the traditional conception is based on the same textual material.

In rereading the chroniclers it is well-worth attempting to see what they said literally, and trying to be free of the many centuries of interpretive overlay. I owe to Dr. Paul Kirchhoff a singularly convincing demonstration of the applicability of literal reading to historical documents in the Americanist field.

The contrast between a literal reading of a particular text and a common interpretation follows:

Joseph Bram, in his book on Inca militarism, tells us that "all private travelling was strictly prohibited by the Incas." [22] In demonstration of this he quotes his source, Bartolomé de las Casas, as follows:

It has been ordered that no Indian should go from one province to another without the knowledge, permission or order of his lords, governors or superiors; and those who disobeyed and travelled without permission were punished very strictly.

This does not say anywhere that all private traveling was strictly prohibited. It says, on the contrary, that knowledge, permission *or* orders were necessary. This means that private travel *was permitted* under the named conditions. Even in our modern period of restricted international communication, can one say that international travel is "strictly prohibited" merely because one requires a passport and a visa, that is, permission?

In defense of Bram, it should be said that his is the usual way in which the quoted passage from De las Casas is interpreted. But it is, nevertheless, an unfortunate distortion.

More basic questions than travel have been dealt with in as cavalier a manner by equally responsible persons. For example, virtually every source and text on the Inca says that in the Inca Empire land was divided among the Inca, the Sun, and the communities. Careless inference has led to such errors as that found in the summary by Dr. Julian Steward in the *Handbook of South American Indians*, where he states that Inca land was "divided into thirds" among these holders.[23] Dr. Steward again is not alone in this reading,[24] but the very chroniclers who made the initial statement go on to give evidence that the land generally was *not* equally divided among the three holders mentioned.

This is a simple mistake. More subtle ones have been as important. Distortions are not hard to find in the interpretation of the material on Inca government, particularly as it depends very much on an understanding of Inca land organization. Lands are usually thought of as of two types:

(1) tax lands:

   plots worked for the Inca (government);

   plots worked for the Sun (national religion).

(2) community lands:

   lands held in common by the agricultural villagers and worked for themselves.

Fitting onto this land basis is the supposed Inca creation of a hierarchy of governing officials who were supported out of the government storehouses. At the head of the country was the divine emperor, possessing absolute power. Under him and implementing his commands were the heads of the four divisions of the empire; beneath these, a hierarchy of officials, having in their jurisdictions respectively 10,000, 5,000, 1,000, 100, 50, and 10 taxpayers and their families. It is usually stated that all taxes were paid in labor, and that in every hamlet land was divided among the Inca, the Sun, and the community. Community lands were divided annually among the taxpayers in proportion to the size of their families. The taxpayers worked the Inca and Sun lands as part of their tax obligation. They could be drafted for other labor or army service as the government required. Through a census system, the tax and administrative structure were kept in balance. Land was inalienable. The picture is immobile.

This version of the land system and its strong political consequences disintegrates alarmingly if touched. Within the pages of the very chronicles which paint this scene, there is other information which suggests that a complex system of land rights and political jurisdiction underlay these grand categories, and that the famous bureaucracy may well be, at least partly, a myth.

The chroniclers tell a different story from the classic one if read with the lawyer's appetite for detail. Lawyers are aware of how clumsy any semantic machinery is to state a rule of law. They have a sorry practical familiarity with the enormous difference between form and substance in political organization. For theoretical equipment the lawyer has the fundamental social emphasis of W. N. Hohfeld's concept that all legal relations are between human beings and that there can be no legal relationship between a person and a thing.[25]

The material on Inca law is too fragmentary to permit it all to be framed in Hohfeld's exact diagnostic terms. Whose demand-right has its counterpart in the duty of another? Whose privilege-right was balanced by the no demand-right of another? In what relations were the reciprocal pairs, power and liability, and immunity and no power, balanced? It is the very search for the precise information which this conception of legal relations requires, that makes Inca law and government appear in unconventional color and dimension.

From the division of beneficial interests and political power over tax produce, the functioning land law can be seen. The exaggerated importance usually given the nominal division of lands among the Inca, the Sun, and the communities has obscured the more basic subdivision of these lands, and has given a spurious impression of unified exploitative control by national Inca institutions. It has also obscured the important but troublesome evidence that there were lands separately held by the families of hereditary government officials.

There is strong evidence that the completely government-supported Inca bureaucracy so often admired may not have existed. Allusions to the *curaca's*[26] lands suggest this. Evidence from which government support of officials can be inferred must not be considered in isolation. Full weight must be given to the fact that government offices were almost all hereditary. This being so, the allusions to *curaca's* lands must then be understood to refer to a specific part of local land, the rights to which were handed down with the office. There is no escaping hereditary official land rights, whether the lands are considered to be entailed in the official's family, or whether they are thought of as attached to the office.

Not only were lands in this sense owned by the *curacas,* but *curaca* landholding appears to have been under quite different conditions in various parts of the empire. In the Inca pattern, which is the one commonly described, the *curaca's* land was worked much as the lands of the Inca and the Sun were worked —by the community he governed as part of a tax obligation. The community held lands of its own and no one but the community had any right to the produce of communal lands. This pattern does not appear to have prevailed throughout the empire. There is evidence that in certain northern coastal valleys, the noble ruler of a valley owned all the land and had tenants who paid him a certain percentage of their produce.[27] The difference in the landholding system between the apparently feudal coastal valleys of the north and the parts of the empire which had the independent communal type of tenure was probably due to the historical past of the areas. The north coast had been a part of the extensive Chimu (or Chimor) kingdom which the Inca conquered in the latter half of the 15th century.[28] A highly developed state, it is not surprising that its land tenure system should have differed from the Inca and that it should have survived the Inca conquest.

The conception of an Inca bureaucracy vanishes and that of a local landed nobility takes its place when evidence of the *curaca* lands is given its proper importance. The persistence of a separate pattern for the Chimu suggests, as does the evidence, that the Inca conquerors were not the land system reformers they are sometimes thought to be.

The writers on the Inca have all described the hierarchy of Inca government officials in very nearly the same terms: the number of government officers depended upon the number of taxpayers counted in multiples of ten. There was thus an official for every 100, every 1,000, every 5,000, every 10,000 taxpayers, etc. But the crucial importance of certain officials who were outside this hierarchy, and the significant differences in power and position of the persons on the decimal government ladder have been inadequately emphasized. Detailed study destroys the neat picture, as in the case of land organization. When the powers and obligations of each rank are examined and the source of income of officials is closely investigated, and when the hereditary nature and local ties of most offices are considered, the decimal system of ranking ceases to appear as a modern salaried bureaucracy and begins to look more like a landed aristocracy.

The Inca incorporated the rulers they conquered into their system of government—a remarkable achievement. But the decimal system and the bureaucracy are an abstraction emphasizing only the central connections of the ruling ranks. One has only to examine local power to see that the office holders of conquered kingdoms became part of the Inca system without losing their identity as local rulers.

A plan of government or of law is an abstraction. It is not the plan alone but the way it functions in practice that matters. Where there is a problem of historical reconstruction, as with the Inca state, the plan is more definite, more compact, more simple, and more consistent than the scrambled odd facts of practice. This study is focused on the workings of the Inca political system and law, and has tried to piece together the scraps of information that show where the practice follows or departs from what is usually inferred from the plan.

One has only to think of the nature of constitutional law where there is a written constitution, as in the United States, to see the problem. For over 175 years the Constitution, a relatively short document, has been the fundamental plan of United States government and law. Yet no one would suggest that this government and this law have been the same for 175 years, though the document itself has hardly changed. Nor would anyone say that an adequate understanding of our government and law could be gleaned from a reading of the Constitution alone.

If the Inca plan of government is thought of in these terms, one can see it in its place. The plan becomes not a description of the Inca government, but an abstraction—the Inca conception of their government structure on its grandest scale. The plan omits more than it includes, if one is seeking a historical description of the Inca political and legal system. It is the purpose of this book to try to reconstruct from the fragments of information in the Spanish sources what is missing in the idealized scheme.

I • THE LAND, THE FORMS OF TENURE

The tendency to attribute the general state of affairs in the empire to the Inca kings is often found in the chronicles. This view was shared both by writers who thought them great social planners and by those who thought them evil despots. The chroniclers found confirmation in what they chose to emphasize of the system of land tenure. In the communally held agricultural lands they saw a form of paternalistic arranging for the masses; in the lands of the Inca and Sun they saw empire-wide support of the central state and national religion; and in the general inalienability of land they saw the strong hand of Inca law.

CENTRAL GOVERNMENT CONTROL AND THE
LAND TENURE SYSTEM

The judgment of the chroniclers on land tenure may well have been colored by the inflated claims of the Spanish kings as successors to the powers and property of the Inca. Some of it may have been lack of political sophistication. Recent writers who choose to see in the Inca régime a form of state socialism, also have made use of these exaggerations of Inca power as it suits their theoretical position.

Most early descriptions of Inca government, and more recent evaluations which try to place the Inca culture in some comparative sociological framework have had, in consequence, strong motives for assuming enormous imperial power. Thus, while Baudin, for example, does not suggest that the collectivism found in the agricultural communities was the creation of

a central government—this much he attributes to "natural evolution"—he all but attributes the rest of the culture to Inca
state activity: an attempt to rationalize society and to absorb
the individual into the state.[1]

It is true that the landholding system was quite static. There
were a few permissible types of land transfer. There appears to
have been no general buying and selling of land interests. Ricardo Latcham [2] believes that the phenomenon of purchase and
sale did exist. He cites a lawsuit brought in 1560 in which many
witnesses testified to a sale of land which had allegedly taken
place in pre-Hispanic times between two *curacas*. In the course
of the present study no evidence of pre-Conquest sales of land
has been found. The record of the case Latcham cites was not
available for examination. If purchase and sale of land were
practiced, it is curious that the chroniclers have not made more
of it. One also wonders what lands the *curacas* might have held
that they could sell—land that was not bound by entailment.

As for the rental of lands, there is some evidence of it in what
seems to be a feudal type of tenancy. In some valleys of the
north coast, in the area of the pre-Inca Chimu kingdom, the
ruling lords owned all the land and had agricultural tenants
who paid them a part of their produce.[3] Other mention of
leasing or rental of lands has not been found in the course of
this research, nor would it seem to fit into the communal agricultural structure.

Leaving aside the north coast type of tenancy and Latcham's
instance of a sale, for want of further information, land interests were transferred only on the following conditions:

(1) Certain of them were transferred on conquest, generally
the assignment of lands in each conquered locality to
the Inca and Sun, and in some instances to colonists.

(2) The Inca could grant lands to individuals he favored,
usually as a reward for outstanding services, or confiscate lands for rebellion or crime.

(3) Inheritance was a fundamental form of transfer, and there were some transfers in anticipation of death.

(4) Some land interests shifted with occupation or office.

(5) There were periodic redivisions of community lands held in common.

Thus, land seems to have been generally inalienable except by the Inca emperor.[4] There is nothing in the inalienability which implies that it was in any sense created or legislated by the government. There is no reason to assume—even if there were an edict on the matter—that this was more than an enunciation of general custom. The general inalienability of land might well be used to show that the Inca government was remarkable in that it rested on a relatively primitive economic order, rather than proving that the Inca government was so strong that it instituted the economic system. Rowe, in keeping with many accounts, describes the reorganization of conquered territory as if it were complete, literally from the ground up: "The lands and flocks were divided and marked, storehouses were built, and the labor taxes introduced."[5] However, it is precisely in information suggesting the limited extent to which the Inca reorganized the landholding system that there is a great deal to be learned about the nature of Inca government. Evidence of this is found in connection with all the forms of landholding and taxation, and the manner in which the government was organized and supported.

The outlines of the Inca land system are sufficiently commonplace in history as not to require any unusual explanation. Communal agriculture accompanied by communal tax obligations are familiar from legal systems all over the world. With variations it is imbedded in Anglo-Saxon and Norman law, in the land tenure system of the Pueblo Indians, in Aztec Mexico, and is found in many other societies. Entailed land, land as the property of kin rather than of individuals, land as relatively inalienable, land as something to which the agriculturalist is attached—all of these forms exist with slight variations in many times and places outside the Andean area in the 16th century.

When a new province was conquered by the Inca, what did the victors exact as far as the land was concerned? Did the landholding *system* change basically? There is good ground for the argument that what changed was merely the beneficial ownership of certain properties. Depending upon the source one favors, on conquest either all land was taken by the emperor, who in every village kept some exclusively for the Inca (government) and Sun (religion) and granted out to the community (collective agricultural unit) the use of the rest; [6] or land interests remained as they were, except that some parcels of land were assigned to the Inca and the Sun.[7] There is no argument between these two versions as to the economic reality. They agree about who got what in terms of value. The difference is rather a legalistic one referring to title.

In the first interpretation, all the land was taken by the conquerors and the use of some of it granted out to local populations, for local governments and local religious purposes. On close scrutiny the use which was granted appears to have followed the pre-Inca arrangements. The second version by definition follows this plan also, except as to the lands assigned the Inca and Sun.

To assume that general similarities of land tenure through the empire always were due to governmental fiat, strains credulity. It presumes that the Inca totally reorganized the landholding system through the acquisition and redistribution of all lands. Where it existed, the homogeneity of community structure and land arrangements probably depended far more on general continuities of Andean culture and history than on imperial edicts.

This is pointed up by the evidence that there was a difference in the system of land tenure between the northern coastal valleys which had once belonged to the Chimu kingdom and the rest of the Inca empire. If the Inca were engaged in establishing a uniform system of landholding in the whole empire, presumably the Chimu type of tenancy [8] would not have escaped alteration. There exist other exceptions to the standard community landholding pattern. Whole villages and all they harvested sometimes belonged to a particular god or temple.[9] The same was true of certain lands held by the Inca emperor.

The ordinary village is usually described as a landholding unit which worked its own lands exclusively for its own benefit, and worked as a tax obligation the separate properties of the local *curaca*, the religious establishment (local and national), and the Inca (for local and national public purposes).

It must not be forgotten that there are exceptions to this pattern by which the whole empire is usually characterized, even though the evidence of them consists of such brief statements that they cannot be discussed in comparable detail.

AGRICULTURAL LAND

The Communities. Agricultural lands of the communities were inalienable. They were inherited and held in common by the able-bodied males of the community. These were the "taxpayers" whose rights to shares of land depended on doing tax-labor in the Inca and Sun fields, and other tax service. The annual division [10] of arable land took place according to the rule that all males received shares in proportion to the size of their families. The distribution was handled by a local official. The share of a person absent at sowing time, who was away at the wars or on other official business, was cultivated by the other shareholders. In this case, the absent man or his family received his share though he had neither planted it nor harvested it.[11] However, when a man was no longer able-bodied, either for reasons of ill health or old age, he ceased to be entitled to a share.[12]

To one accustomed to modern American real property concepts, the most striking characteristics of this type of land ownership are its communal nature, the inalienability of the individual's land interest, and the further connection between work and property interest. Except for those away on official business only those who cultivated had a share.

In referring to a communal landholding unit the sources sometimes use the word "*ayllu*." Rowe defines the *ayllu* as "a kin group with theoretical endogamy, with descent in the male line [which] owned a definite territory." [13] Whatever one's opinion of the extent of actual endogamy as opposed to theoretical endogamy, or actual kinship as opposed to theoretical kinship, these elements were surely present to some extent in the landholding unit. (Probably there was local variation to confuse matters still further.) Suffice it to say that there are indications that there were binding social ties in the communities as well as the economic bonds involved in communal landholding.

The annual readjustment of shares of communal lands has been interpreted as an adjustment to need—evidence of the benevolent social planning of the Inca government. Such an interpretation assumes an unnecessary degree of paternalism and also the historically improbable factor that the communal land system originated in the imperial will.

Where there was a land shortage, shares adjusted according to family size may have been related to need, though not necessarily to Inca planning. Where there was an abundance of land, the number of people in a family might nevertheless have had some importance in relation to the quantity of land that could be worked. Polo mentions the number of workers in a family as well as the number who had to be fed.[14] In the Incaic social arrangement, where additional labor could not be acquired by the ordinary household, only the amount of land that a family could work by itself had any value. There were no slaves, tenant farmers, or other laborers to be had by the agriculturalist-taxpayer class.

The communities lived as units, away from the terraces and

fields. Hence the annual redistribution of arable land did not force families to move their homes. Rowe has suggested that the annual redivision might have been related to crop rotation.[15] One may assume that the readjustment of shares also was a consideration.

Lands Held by an Individual Grantee. Both Polo and Cobo,[16] —the latter doubtless following the former—distinguish from community holdings lands granted to individuals by the Inca. Such lands were given as a reward for outstanding services in war, or engineering (construction of a bridge or road is mentioned), or to the sons of nobles who served in the Inca emperor's household, or, says Polo, for other reasons.

These lands were given in perpetuity to the grantee and to his descendants in common. They could neither divide it nor alienate it. The senior kinsman held it as head of the *ayllu,* but all male descendants enjoyed the fruits. Such lands were divided for cultivation at sowing time. The division was made by the head of the *ayllu* and lineage, as senior kinsman, *per capita* among the male descendants present. The right to a designated share at the time of sowing was permanent. If a man entitled to a share did not appear at sowing time, he did not receive his part of the harvest, nor could he assign his share to a substitute. But no matter how long his absence, his right to a share was not lost. It could be reasserted. Most of the lands held under these conditions were said to be in the neighborhood of Cuzco.

Before giving examples of instances in which "reward" land was granted, both Polo and Cobo state that no one could own any land individually without having it by grace of the Inca. This has probably led to the common assumption that these "rewards" were the only instances of land held by individuals in the Inca empire. This would seem to be incorrect, for Cobo [17] speaks elsewhere of the *curaca's* (government officials below the rank of Inca provincial governor) lands, and so do a substantial number of other sources.[18]

It is noteworthy that the "reward" lands mentioned should have been found principally in the neighborhood of Cuzco, the capital of the Inca empire, and the area from which the Inca people expanded. Also significant is the fact that they seem to have been cultivated by the owners, since presence at sowing time was requisite for sharing in the harvest. Were these lands principally granted to people in the agriculturalist class, persons who were also entitled to a share of community land? Polo's statement of the matter could be interpreted this way, particularly since the nobility, the governing officials of substantial rank, did no agricultural work.

The Sun Lands. Cobo and Polo tell us that wherever there were towns or villages with agricultural lands, there were some local lands designated as the Sun's and some as the Inca's.[19] The three land units, the Sun, the Inca, and the community are often spoken of by the chroniclers as if they constituted a complete picture of the Inca land tenure system. However, all the implications that seem to flow from this tripartite division do not actually follow. The apparently sharp differentiation between national ownership and local community holdings becomes far less clear on close examination.

This is dramatically true in the case of lands of the Sun. Since they are named according to the national Inca religion, it is important to note that the produce from these lands was by no means entirely directed toward a national institution, nor toward its local branches. It was to a significant extent, locally consumed and applied to local institutions. Nor were the Sun lands a single undivided unit. To quote Rowe's translation of Cobo: [20]

The lands dedicated to the gods were divided among the Sun, Lightning, and the other idols, shrines and guacas of general worship or restricted to the province or town; the amount belonging to each god and guaca was specified.[21]

What was gathered was put in local storehouses, in part for sacrifices and in part for the support of the *huaca* attendants.[22]

Some of what was not used locally was taken to the provincial capital and some to Cuzco, the center of the most important deities. Acosta says that the largest part went to Cuzco.[23] Recalling that the Inca conquerors transported the most important local idols to Cuzco, and that persons from these localities served in Cuzco as attendants of their gods,[24] one may infer that some of the local produce going to Cuzco went for the support of these persons and shrines,[25] as well as for the national sanctuaries.

Within the communities themselves, there were persons who took care of and attended the local *huacas,* and a piece of land was designated for their support.[26] These *huaca* attendants did not do agricultural work. Polo tells us that they were persons too old or otherwise unable to work, and that they would have been dependent on the community in any case. The number of attendants varied according to the size of the community.

These lands might as easily be called "community *huaca* lands" as "Sun lands." Their produce was consumed in sacrifices to local gods and in the support of their attendants from generation to generation. They were not inheritable in the sense of passing from individual to individual. They were passed on to disabled and aged persons within the community, from generation to generation, in just as real a sense as the right to a share in community lands. In spite of the fact that they were called "Sun lands," would the Inca "church" have had the temerity to take away the local *huaca* lands for national purposes—even were there a theoretical right? It seems very doubtful.

The poor are said by Valera to have been supported out of Sun storehouses.[27] Whether this refers to *huaca* attendants or to other persons is not clear. Other sources say they were supported out of the Inca storehouses.[28] Both may be true. There seems no doubt that there were people who, by reason of not being in the family of an able-bodied man, or being able to work themselves, were supported by the community. Care of these persons seems to have been managed through some local consumption of Inca and Sun produce by community dependents. Whether there were other "lands of the poor" is not clear. They are referred to simply as such by Garcilaso,[29] and by Castro and Ortega Morejón.[30]

In the provincial capitals, the temple of the Sun and the "House of the Chosen Women" were establishments supported by the agricultural labors of the whole province.[31] A good part of the produce of the Sun lands went for this purpose.[32] One might well suppose that the produce of Sun lands supported the labor necessary for the building of whatever local temples were constructed. Certain temples apparently held lands as such.[33] Cobo and Polo tell us that in some places there were whole villages, which together with all they harvested belonged to the Sun and other gods.[34] This sounds quite different from the more usual community which held its own lands and cultivated separate tax lands.

Lands of the Sun then were not simply a great block of fields or terraces belonging to the "Empire Church." They were subdivided into small plots whose produce was allocated for many local purposes and local deities, only a part going to provincial capitals and to Cuzco, to support the official national religion of the realm. The Spanish effort to eradicate and replace all indigenous religions seems to have led to the assumption that the Inca attempted the same *vis à vis* local cults.[35] On the contrary, the Sun cult appears to have been simply superimposed on local cults. As Bram tells us, the religion of the Sun vanished with the Inca, and the principal struggle of the Catholic church was not against the Inca national religion, but against local cults.[36]

It is not difficult to see how the continued support of pre-Inca-conquest religions and the super-imposition of the Sun cult was possible on a property basis. The "Sun lands" maintained both. Their misleading designation as "Sun lands," like so many of the chroniclers terms, has simplified the picture and distorted it. Examination of the legal arrangement in the empire, both from a landholding and a tax standpoint gives a more realistic conception.

Lands of Officials Other Than the Inca Governors. There are many allusions to lands associated with official positions.[37] Official posts were hereditary above the lowest decimal ranks, but subject always to the question of fitness. No *curaca,* including and above the rank of centurion, did agricultural labor.[38] Statements abound that the *curacas'* lands were worked by the community.[39] This aspect of landholding and cultivation may have been pre-Incaic.[40]

Cobo's statements and those of the others simply assume that where there were Inca and Sun and community lands, the *curacas* also had specific lands. Garcilaso says so explicitly. Yet Valera says the *curacas* from centurion up had their needs provided for from the royal storehouses.[41] Rowe adopts this view,[42] and indeed it is the traditional way to describe the Inca administration. But there seems strong ground for doubting that this was the case. Santillán speaks of the assigning of lands to the *curacas* as one of the duties of the provincial governor (*t'oqrikoq*).[43] The many direct references in the major sources mentioned to "working the *curacas* lands" cannot be overridden easily, nor can the fact that in describing the use made of the produce in Inca storehouses, the support of *curacas* is not mentioned.[44]

Was the *curaca's* land then simply a share of the community land? There is an ambiguous passage in Cobo describing communal distribution which says that no one, whether noble or plebeian, was given more land than was necessary to support himself and his family.[45] But it would seem an extension of meaning to say that this by itself means that *curaca's* lands were a part of community lands. Other evidence turns one away from this interpretation.

First there is the matter of historical events to consider. The

Inca kept local officials in office when they conquered an area.[46] Are we to assume that the Inca took away their lands, or that they had none? Neither is easy to believe. And if one of these alternatives is taken to be true, what are we to make of the numerous allusions to working *curacas* lands mentioned above?

Garcilaso would have us believe that the amount of land under cultivation was everywhere so increased by Inca technology that no one was deprived of what he held previously.[47] This may have been true in some regions, but surely the Andean area in general shared the agricultural techniques of the Inca. One would judge from the Chincha Valley material that on conquest the *curacas* assigned a piece of community land from each valley to the Inca,[48] and kept other lands for themselves. To the same general effect Santillán[49] says that on conquest the *curaca* of each province gave native lands to the Inca and Sun, and that the previous owners were still known in his day.

A particular instance in which the *curaca* individually owned lands is described in the *Relaciones geográficas*. In certain coastal valleys (*yungas*) the *cacique* (hispanization of *curaca*) owned all the land and his subjects were simultaneously his tenants. These tenants paid the *cacique* a share of what they harvested.[50] In telling us that all these lands were the individual property of the *cacique*, the chronicler notes that this system was exceptional in the Inca empire, and mentions the communal landholding pattern as prevalent elsewhere.

Since "yunga" was the Quechua word for the language spoken in the northern half of the pre-Inca kingdom of Chimor,[51] it would seem quite reasonable to assume that these are the valleys alluded to. The probability that a feudal arrangement existed in part (if not all) of the Chimor kingdom, and that it persisted through the Inca conquest to the Spanish Conquest is of considerable historical interest. Not only does it fit in very well with the survival of Chimor dynasties and the persistence of other local cultural characteristics,[52] but it also suggests a good deal about the Inca empire itself. For one thing it shows that even as to so basic a matter as a landholding system, there probably was no complete homogeneity in the empire. It strongly suggests that the Inca left the landholding system as they found it in conquered areas. They took property for themselves, to be sure, but probably did not alter the basic land structure.

Still another mention of land individually owned by *curacas* is made by Polo when speaking of certain coca plantations.[53] Santillán speaks of gathering the coca of the Incas and the *curacas*.[54] While some sources say that coca was an Inca monopoly, the statements of Polo and Santillán are well worth considering.[55] The *curacas* also appear to have controlled local mines.[56]

These examples tend to confirm what the many allusions to working the *curacas'* lands imply—namely that the *curacas* held separate properties of their own.

The detailed account of the Chincha and neighboring valleys states this clearly.[57] There lands were inherited with the office of *curaca* only when the successor in office belonged to the same "pachaca" or 100. The lands of the *curaca* were not alienable, nor could they be diminished in value in any respect by an incumbent. On the contrary, they were to be added to. They constituted a kind of entailed estate, which provided all that was necessary for the sons of the preceding *curaca,* as well as for the incumbent in office. It is said that the *curacas* were rich by reason of the estate being kept entire and added to.

The quantity of land held by the *curacas* and leaders of 100 or 1,000 was not fixed: some held 20 *hanegas*,[58] others 12 or less.[59] The irregular distribution is said to date from the first Inca, Tupac Yupanqui, from whose time there was supposed to have been no alteration in the distribution of agricultural lands (*chacaras*).

The material on the Chincha Valley could not be construed

to mean that the *curaca* shared in the annual communal distribution, nor does it suggest in any way that the *curaca's* land was a designated segment of Inca land allocated for local government. On the contrary, the material, particularly that on the Chincha Valley, shows that the *curaca's* lands were separate from community and Inca land; and that the office carried with it the right to have the *curaca's* lands worked by the people the *curaca* governed.

Inca tax stores, then, did not support the *curacas*. Neither did they invariably support the Inca's emissaries. This is indicated by the same account of the Chincha Valley.[60]

Castro says that in the Chincha Valley the Inca government official (*tocorico, sayapaya* or *micho*) was fed and clothed by the *curacas* of the valley, but that their fields were elsewhere.[61] This last seems to refer to visiting rather than resident officials, and the *tocorico* was probably the inspector (*tokoy-rikoq*) rather than the governor.[62] Bandera elsewhere describes the *micho* as an aide of the governor [63] stationed in every major town. It is interesting that they should have been, so to speak, guests of the *curacas*, rather than living on local Inca government stores. It would certainly have served the *curacas'* interest to care personally for the comforts of those who inspected their districts. This also speaks for the personal resources of the *curacas*.

One treads particularly cautiously in the matter of *curaca* lands because of the apparent inconsistency with the tripartite division of land among the Inca, Sun, and communities. *Curaca* lands do not fit into this neat picture, but many sources seem inescapably to point to their existence. Not only did *curaca* lands apparently exist, but the material on the Chincha Valley and on the Chimor kingdom suggests that *curacas* held lands under quite different conditions in two parts of the empire. It is difficult to infer anything other than that *curaca* lands did exist quite generally. They were not solely created by gifts of the Inca to reward his followers, but seem to have been the properties of conquered *curacas*—properties which were not taken away through Inca conquest, but were left to their owners.

Lands of the Inca Governors. Information on the lands of the Inca governors suggests that the heads of provinces had interest in at least two and possibly three distinct types of property:

(1) lands near Cuzco which had descended in their families since they were *orejones* of Inca lineage;

(2) discretion over the expenditure of the produce of Inca lands;

(3) possible personal fields in the province they governed.

As for (1) most of the governors, Cieza reports, had their hereditary lands in the Cuzco region.[64]

With respect to (2) the evidence is also fairly clear. The fact that the governor had charge of Inca and Sun lands in his province is stated in a number of places.[65] One can infer that this involved more than mere tax collection and included discretion over the local expenditure of Inca and Sun tax stores.

Cobo, in speaking of the amount of tax taken to Cuzco from the Inca and Sun storehouses, says that care was taken to see that the provincial capitals remained adequately provisioned for ordinary expenses and current needs.[66] Ordinary expenses seem to have been rather large.[67]

Did the provincial governor derive most of his income from these Inca and Sun tax lands within his province? It seems possible. The office of governor was created by Inca conquest, and Inca and Sun lands were conquest acquisitions. The relative newness of the position of governor is in contrast to that of the *curacas* whose landholdings, just as their rights to government office, appear to have been hereditary and to have antedated the Inca invasion.

The post of Inca governor may not have been inheritable. Information is lacking. Most administrative positions below the rank of governor were hereditary subject to the question of fitness. There was a tendency toward inheritability in the higher offices as well as to both the Inca-ship and the position of the four viceroys. If the governor's position did not tend to be inheritable, it was the only office in the decimal administrative system not to be so. In that case, the governor's interest in the produce of Inca and Sun lands would present the only possible bureaucratic "salary" in the system. On the other hand; if there existed a tendency to choose the governor's successor from among his brothers or sons, the interest in these tax lands would be somewhat analogous to an entailed property interest.

As for (3) the knotty question of whether the governors held personal lands in the provinces they governed—there is some evidence that they did. Murúa [68] specifically speaks of the fields of the governor. Cobo [69] tells us that the governors and certain other high ranking Inca officials and their sons were supported by the tribute of personal service which was given them by the taxpayers. At the rate of one *mita* worker for every 100 taxpayers governed, the governor had a personal staff of 400.[70] When Cobo again discusses [71] the economic support of the administrative hierarchy from governor down, he says that the taxpayers worked the lands of the officials. This sounds distinctly as if they had lands in the province. The text does not specify the governors nor except them, but lumps the whole government officialdom together. There is evidence in the taxation system that officials had resources with which to support craftsmen. The governor regularly presented craft objects to the Inca emperor as gifts. It would seem a contradiction if these "gifts" were produced by craftsmen supported by Inca lands.[72] This also suggests private resources for the provincial governor in the province he ruled.

One cannot conclude absolutely that the Inca governor had private lands in his province, nor that his family had an enduring economic interest in local Inca and Sun lands. The evidence is insufficient. But there is no doubt that the Inca governor had a stake in what was produced in his province. Governing on behalf of the Inca emperor, to be sure, the *t'oqrikoq* also governed in his own interest. His tenure may have depended on his ability to extract taxes. What is more, if the magnificence of his capital and the embellishment of his own life depended on what was produced on Inca and Sun land in the Inca's name, how much more diligent may he have been in enforcing provincial taxes, and how strong his personal economic interest in what he governed?

Inca Lands. The assumption runs through the literature that Inca lands were of only one sort, namely a segment of national tax-land set aside in each community to support the government. But this is not the whole story. It would seem that there were at least two types of Inca lands:

(1) family lands which descended in the various Inca lineages;

(2) local segments of tax-land throughout the empire designated as Inca lands, but in fact used for a variety of tax purposes including many local public expenditures.

Cieza tells us that the Inca governors held lands in the Cuzco region which had descended in their families since they were *orejones* of Inca lineage.[73] He also tells us that the sons of the Inca other than those by his official wife were provided with lands of their own.[74] These lands were probably entailed since this seems to have been the only form of ownership by an individual used in the Inca empire. That there were lands of the Inca which supported his womenfolk, family retainers, and shrine after his death is also clearly stated by Cieza.[75]

The same source says that the service of Incas themselves in the royal fields near Cuzco was by the *yanaconas*—retainers for life very much like slaves.[76] It would appear then, that the Inca's own fields, as opposed to tax-lands, were not cultivated through *mita* service. The mention of *yanacona*-cultivated personal fields near Cuzco, and the material on the maintenance of the Inca's fields after death by his retainers,[77] is hard to understand except in the context of the ruling Inca's personal possessory interest in specific non-government lands. Some of this land was apparently obtained by confiscating it from rebellious members of the nobility, and the local commoners were made *yanaconas*.[78]

Without questioning the fact that the financing of most Inca projects depended on Inca tax-fields, Cieza's material strongly suggests that there were lands owned by the Inca in a more individual sense. What else could lands be, which on the Inca's death continued to be worked by his retainers for their own support and that of his relatives and for his shrine? The Inca also must have controlled lands he was free to grant. The Inca granted lands to reward individuals for special services in war, government, and engineering.[79] Land grants also seem to have been given the sons of *curacas* who served the Inca well.[80] Are we to believe that the Inca granted lands to individuals for worthy service, to engineers, warriors and the like, but that he and his kith and kin depended entirely on the Inca tax-lands scattered throughout the empire? Cieza and Cabello suggest otherwise.

The Inca government fields found in each community are commonly cited in support of the theory that there was a government-supported bureaucracy. Rowe has said (as has Valera) that the *curacas* were supported by the income from the government fields,[81] but considerable evidence has been cited here to the contrary.[82]

Though the *curacas* seem not to have been supported by Inca fields, the produce was nevertheless much divided. It went in part to Cuzco; in part to support the provincial capital; [83] in part to care for traveling armies and officials as they passed through; [84] in part to maintain newly settled *mitimaes*,[85] probably to support the local population when road work was undertaken,[86] and to maintain some of the poor [87] and people too old to do agricultural labor.

Though the produce of Inca fields was divided, the lands

themselves do not appear to have been divided in the way that the lands of the Sun were. Indeed, division would have been impractical. The allocation of produce from Inca fields does not seem to have involved a stable division of income. Rather it depended on what projects happened to be running at the time.

There is a puzzling description of Inca lands in Castro and Ortega Morejón's "Relación" on the Chincha Valley. Lands of the first Inca, the second Inca etc. are said to have been distinct, and to have been irrigated and cultivated in that order.[88] What did this mean? Were Inca lands the property of the crown, or did each Inca have his own lands, which on his death supported his relatives and retainers and his shrine? Can the tax-fields possibly have been involved in the tradition that the Inca emperors did not inherit from their predecessors? Did each Inca in turn extend the tax-lands? Was this division of lands found only in the Chincha Valley or elsewhere as well? Were these the private lands of the Inca as opposed to the tax-lands?

What is certain is that the produce of Inca tax-fields was very much divided. It was a kind of capital on which the Inca, and probably his governors, could draw to finance national and provincial projects of construction and other undertakings.

The fact that there were Inca family estates is parallel to the fact that the Inca storehouses were not used to support the whole governing hierarchy, but that most officials also held family fields. These family holdings place Inca economics, government, and law in a rather different light from more usual interpretations. The frequent emphasis on national institutions to the exclusion of others would seem to be rather unsound.

The Relative Quantities of Inca, Sun, and Community Lands. One could say that land in the United States today is divided into two parts, government owned and privately owned. Although true enough as far as it goes, this does not tell very much about actual circumstances of land tenure and law. Neither does the conventional tripartite division of land tenure under the Inca.

Subtleties of interest and control might have gone without saying for the Inca. Gross classifications might well have been adequate to those entirely familiar with the realities of power. But to us of another era, these classifications will not do.

Some writers have pursued these classifications in an extreme fashion. They have added the further ingredient of equality, and have interpreted the chroniclers' statements about the land being divided into three parts to mean that in each locality the land was divided into thirds.[89] Rowe apparently does not subscribe to the division into thirds, since he quotes Cobo in full.[90]

As to agricultural land, the chroniclers indicate that there was no general rule about the relative extent of lands allocated to the three nominal holders.[91] These sources tell us that the division was irregular—that in some places in the empire all the land was of the Sun and other gods, and that elsewhere the share of the Inca was very large. Acosta and Cobo tell us that Inca storehouses were everywhere larger than those of the Sun, however, which suggests that Inca lands were more extensive.[92]

If all the lands of a particular area were "of the Sun" one wonders what position the resident agriculturalists occupied. What was their relation to the land as compared with that of persons in other areas where community lands existed? A similar question arises in the case of the north coast valleys in which the local *cacique* is said to have owned all the land.[93] And what of the Inca and Sun lands in areas where the *cacique* owned all the land?

In the Chincha Valley, there was land allocated to the Inca in each 1,000-taxpayer unit (*guaranga*). While the precise extent of the Inca property varied from one unit to the next,[94] it does not seem to have been more than a small proportion of the land cultivated for community use.

Departing for a moment into the dubious realm of measurement: [95] Castro and Ortega Morejón tell us that the amount of Inca land per *guaranga* was "10 *hanegas de sembradura*" and in some cases more.[96] Valera equates *fanega* with *tupu*—the amount of land received by every taxpayer for himself and his wife.[97] In a *guaranga* the minimum community holdings (excluding the amounts additional to a *tupu* granted for children) would be 1,000 *tupus*. Assuming *hanega* and *fanega* to be variant spellings of the same word, and equivalent to a *tupu*, Inca lands in the *guaranga* would be only 10 *tupus* while community holdings would be well over 1,000. The Inca lands by this calculation were no more than 1 percent of the land cultivated by the Indians for themselves, considerably less than 1 percent if one includes *tupus* for children. This may be compared with the statement that two thirds of the agricultural produce went to the Sun and Inca and one third remained to the communities.[98] It is also interesting to consider how the Inca share of "10 *hanegas*" compared with that stated for the *curaca's* of 100 and 1,000 which varied from fewer than 12 to 20 *hanegas*.[99] This description would indicate that more land was cultivated for the local rulers than for the Inca.

On conquest of an area the amount of land assigned to the Inca may have depended in some measure upon the circumstances of victory or capitulation. Since local rulers were not removed, their tenure depended to some extent upon their cooperation with the conqueror; the quantity of land ceded to the Inca might have varied with the bargaining positions of the local authorities.

There also must have been considerable variations in the productivity of land—thus area-extent alone would not necessarily have governed the allocation. Castro and Ortega Morejón place on this ground the variation from *guaranga* to *guaranga* of the size of Inca holdings.[100]

Garcilaso would have us believe that the Inca enlarged the cultivable lands of each conquered province through the skills of his irrigation engineers and thus tax lands did not really diminish local property.[101] Because Garcilaso was so anxious to show Inca benevolence, one may question whether he is to be believed on this point.

PROPERTY INTERESTS IN
OTHER THAN AGRICULTURAL LAND

Land used for other than agricultural purposes was often held on other conditions. Pasture lands are described by Cobo and Polo as being divided among the Inca, the Sun, and the communities,[102] and their flocks are said to have been pastured on their respective lands.[103] Yet there were evidently privately owned flocks as well [104] and one may wonder where these were pastured. Santillán tells us that all the *caciques* held a certain number of head. From Cobo one can infer that privately owned animals were pastured with the community herds. The governing officials as well as the community itself might then have shared property interests in the community pastures.

All the hunting grounds and woodlands are said to have belonged to the Inca.[105] They were divided among the provinces but were not otherwise subdivided as were the pasture lands. Although nominally Inca-owned, these lands were used by the communities resident in the neighborhood, who needed permission of the Inca, his governors, or possibly lower administrative officers to use the lands for fuel, building materials and hunting. Poma tells us that the penalty for cutting trees or grass without permission was death.[106] Certain game was preserved and not allowed to be hunted, but predatory animals could be killed for the damage they caused.[107] Cobo says that the penalty for hunting without permission was beating with a stone for the first offense and death for the second.[108]

The actual exploitation of hunting grounds and woodlands by the communities has more legal significance than nominal "ownership." There is no reason to believe that because the Inca reserved for himself and for his administrative officers the right to deny the use of woodlands and hunting grounds, that such permission was not regularly granted. It seems far more likely that the communities continued to use these lands in much the same way after as before the Incaic conquest.

The property rights of the Inca in the woodlands and hunting grounds can be seen as subject to customary general use. Administrative supervision was probably to insure that community consumption would not appreciably decrease the upper class supply of fuel, wood, and game. The royal hunts [109] appear to have been the most striking form of Inca exploitation of these lands. Thus, despite the fact that Cobo and Polo say that the woodlands and hunting grounds belonged to the Inca, such property interest as they had must be seen in the light of commonly exercised community rights as well.

Water rights must have been closely associated with land rights and virtually as important in those parts of Peru which were irrigated. Cobo tells us [110] that local officials had charge of determining land and water distribution. In the Chincha Valley it is said that the Inca fields were watered first.[111] The theft of water by directing it to one's own fields out of turn was a punishable offense.[112]

Clearly defined rights to water obviously existed. The criminal theft of water indicates this. Yet water rights are not discussed by the chroniclers in terms of property. One does not find it stated that "all the water belonged to the Inca," or any part of it to anyone.

The rights to salt, salubrious fountains, sea water, fish in rivers and streams, and wild fruits were also locally regulated.[113] Valera says these rights were common to the natives of the respective provinces where they occurred.

Mining rights present still another set of relationships. Statements do exist to the effect that all the mines did belong to the Inca.[114] Other accounts, however, show instances of control by the caciques which do not seem consonant with total Inca ownership. Cobo, for instance,[115] speaks of most mines being worked for the benefit of the *caciques* of the districts in which the mines were located. The local leaders, he says, used the products for gifts to the Inca.[116] That there were mines controlled by the local *caciques* rather than by the Inca is confirmed by Valera [117] and somewhat corroborated by Las Casas.[118] Garcilaso says that gold and silver mines were granted to the *curacas*.[119]

These sources describe a local, rather than a national control and exploitation of gold and silver mines. Nothing has been discovered in this study which refers specifically to copper mining. Since copper was in general use, and was not restricted by sumptuary laws,[120] and since it was abundant,[121] one may infer that there was still more local control of copper mining. Not even gold and silver were exclusively controlled by the central government, although their use was restricted by sumptuary laws. Copper was very likely mined under local direction and, at least in part, for local benefit.

The roads provide another instance of an over-emphasis on imperial power by the chroniclers. They were all locally maintained, both the two main through highways (the so-called royal roads of Highland and Coast) and the others.[122] But though the royal roads were maintained and possibly originally built by labor from the localities through which they passed, they were essentially an imperial institution with post runners (*chasquis*) and resting and supply houses (*tambos*) at regular intervals. There was also a tremendous network of "non-royal" roads. Some local control is evident from such things as tolls taken in kind from all persons entering or leaving a city.[123] In Xerez's "Relación" there is reference to a guard stationed at the beginning of a bridge on the road to Cajas (near Huancabamba) who received tolls. Atahualpa had the toll suspended for supplies taken to his garrison there. But no one else was exempt, and any other entrance or egress from the city was forbidden on pain of death. Such toll taking also existed at Pachacamac and at Huanuco.[124] But even though tolls existed, there is no indication that they formed any part of royal revenue. On the contrary, it seems quite probable that they were local institutions. Thus, while the central government dealt with the roads for certain purposes, local government maintained them and also exercised a measure of control. The chroniclers do not discuss ownership of roads as such.

From the point of view of modern law a striking omission exists in the lack of concern over the ownership of land on which buildings were erected. This lack of concern does seem consistent with the structure of Inca land law. One can hardly imagine rival claims to the site of a temple or a palace. While frequent mention is made of storehouses of the Inca, the ownership of the land on which the storehouses were built is not specified. The same is true of all buildings, public and private. The land on which they stood is not mentioned, nor its ownership defined. One might assume that the land automatically belonged to the person or institution to which the building belonged. Yet if such were true, it would merely re-emphasize that the ownership of this land was not considered in terms familiar to modern lawyers. The land on which buildings were erected was not the object of competing claims; it was not transferred from a previous owner to a new owner when a building or a city was built. This suggests that urbanization itself had not reached a point where such questions would arise. One gets the impression from the land law material that much of the economically unproductive land was unclaimed. All the land may have been divided for administrative purposes (though one may wonder how approximately this was done), but that it was all owned in any modern sense seems very doubtful indeed.

DISPUTES OVER LAND

In the division of shares of community land, and presumably in the settlement of any disputes arising from this division, the local leader—whether called senior kinsman, *ayllu* head, *cacique,* or *curaca*—performed one of his judicial functions. There seems to have been neither appeal nor escape from his decision.

Polo [125] tells us that in the colonial courts there was hardly a single lawsuit over disputed land pending between individuals. Virtually all suits were brought by groups or pueblos, that is, the holders in common. What then of grants by the Inca to individuals? Had they all passed on to communities of heirs? Polo says that disputes over annual individual shares were disputes with the *cacique.* He did not know of any such arguments brought into the colonial courts. He also tells us that a dispute with the *cacique* over the share assigned was not likely to arise, because at least in the sierras, there was a great surplus of land.[126] We may infer that land was not as abundant elsewhere. Polo indicates that the suits between groups and pueblos which did come up in the colonial courts had to do with the members of a community cultivating lands outside of their community. In this connection he mentions land shortage directly.[127]

Bearing out Polo's report are the corroborating statements of others that most post-Columbian lawsuits between Peruvians concerned the possession of land. These were apparently adjudicated according to indigenous rules.[128] He reports a method that is possibly of pre-Columbian origin. The parties in question being summoned and present, the judge who is to decide the case goes to the disputed lands with neighboring witnesses. Each of the disputants alleges his claim. After testimony, when it has been ascertained to whom the lands belong, an order is given in his favor.[129] These proceedings, described ambiguously, in rather European terms, are anything but detailed. But it may be significant that in this determination of land ownership there is allusion neither to landmarks and maps, nor to supernatural methods of ascertaining the truth.

Disputes over land bring to the fore the question of the setting of landmarks and the mapping of land ownership. The *Relaciones geográficas* tells us that the ancient borders of the town lands were well-known to all indigenous communities, and they were generally acknowledged to be some natural landmark, such as a stream or a hill.[130] Sarmiento tells of maps the Inca had made on conquering an area. Well-known as they may have been, the borders were apparently in constant dispute. In pre-Incaic times it is said that these controversies were settled by wars.[131] In the Inca period the settlement of such questions was probably one of the duties of each governing official in his area. Sometimes it was the occasion for the sending of a special Inca delegate.[132] De las Casas and Cobo relate that under the Inca, landmarks were actually placed at the borders of the towns and provinces.[133] Cobo cites that the penalty for removing landmarks or entering on the land of another was beating with a stone for the first offense and death for the second. He also refers to landmarks delineating the lands of the Inca and the Sun.[134]

The material seems to allude solely to the marking of taxlands and borders between communities and between provinces. It does not refer to the internal division of land within the communities, but to the larger administrative divisions by which the central government taxed and ruled the land, and kept the peace beween towns. In keeping with this, Valera clearly distinguishes between the law which divided the land for administrative purposes among the towns and provinces, and the law which divided the land for agricultural purposes within the communities.[135]

Both the evidence on the practice of setting landmarks and the nature of the disputes brought before Spanish courts [136] suggest a difference in the handling of "public" and "private" disputes about land. The difference we know of resides in the agencies handling such arguments, for we know little of the methods of settlement. The central government intervened in land disputes only in certain matters. It left the absolute decision

of private contentions to local authorities. It can be inferred
that the Inca government was interested in maintaining its
administrative organization and the tax structure which depended on it. Disputes among communities were a threat to
the public peace and served as an opportunity for the central
government to make its strength felt as a higher arbitrating
authority. Disputes between individuals within a community
were not the concern of the Inca central government. They
were a local problem to be handled completely locally. There
was no appeal to a higher authority in such matters. The central
government was in no way involved in the arguments between
individuals over land—unless one regards the local *curaca*
principally as the agent of the Inca government. This view
emphasizes an apparent top-to-bottom unity of Inca government. Yet there was a marked separateness of the sub-units
owing to geographical divisions of exclusive jurisdiction, and
the split between conqueror and conquered.

The Inca government involved a hierarchy of officials with
delegated authority exclusively responsible to the next higher
official on the ladder. Checking was done through periodic
inspections and spying. The activities of lower officials were
reviewed by the higher ones, but this was accomplished
through reports presented by the lower official himself, and
through such information as was available from spies and inspections. This is a rather different arrangement from one in
which the central government reviews the appeals of the
governed, or legislates concerning such disputes, or otherwise
intervenes more directly in private law. Perhaps this intervention in private law arises only when the central government
has a definite interest in the relations of its citizens. For example: If taxes depend on land ownership, the central government may well have an interest in who owns the land. Where
there are taxes on inheritance of land, the central government
has an interest in knowing from whom it will collect the taxes
—that is, in who inherits.

Disputes over land rights could not have affected the Inca central government as long as the public peace was maintained, for its tax system was largely independent of individual land rights. Since the chroniclers were far more interested and informed about the activities of the central government than those of the local *curacas*, such a body of private law as may well have been developed (probably with local variation) has generally escaped their attention. It is difficult to imagine that there were no disputes over annual land redistributions. As has been mentioned, the decision of the *curaca* was final in this matter. His consent may also have legalized the possession of virgin lands.

The same indifference of the central government toward intra-community land quarrels also applied to inheritance. The Inca rulers had no particular gain in standardizing the rules of inheritance throughout the realm. Local variations in determining the heirs did not affect the tax structure. Such variations in inheritance seem to have existed both in pre- and post-Incaic times.[137] Fights for landed property within noble families were probably of interest to the central government only in so far as the loyalty and ability of successors to governing posts were involved. That is, the government was far more concerned with the political consequences of inheritance than in the property aspect.

The absence of all but shreds of information about land disputes between individuals is consistent with the general nature of entailed and communal land tenure. Most quarrels presumably concerned a community or a family, or was settled within one of these units. The lack of information also jibes with the chroniclers' preoccupation with the central government and the presumable indifference of that government to disputes in which it had neither an economic nor a political stake.

In contrast, the interest of the Inca government in administrative and tax geography is very much in keeping with what can be inferred of the plan of empire government. The division of populated areas among the officials of the decimal hierarchy must in theory have settled all major questions of political jurisdiction and the apportionment of taxes. Changes in pre-Inca arrangements must have been a source of considerable irritation to the defeated. The heavy penalties for moving landmarks more than suggests difficulties encountered in enforcing their acceptance.

TITLE AND USUFRUCT AS BETWEEN
THE INCA AND THE COMMUNITIES

There is an old controversy about whether the title to all land belonged to the emperor who granted out the usufruct of part to the communities, or whether title to all land belonged to the communities, which granted the usufruct of a part to the Inca and Sun.

Cobo said that the Inca emperor held title to all lands of the realm.[138] Acosta, Polo, Valera, Santillán and Damian de la Bandera say the land belonged to the communities.[139] Baudin [140] has said the title of the Emperor was at most nominal if it existed at all. Cunow and Trimborn, who emphasize the historical precedence of the communities, consider them the fundamental owners.[141]

The principal reason why opposite views of the matter are tenable is that to all appearances it does not make any practical difference who held the title. This particular conceptualization of split ownership was a European one, which for immediate Spanish interests may have been read back into the Inca land tenure system, rather than being inherent in the Inca conception. It is possible to examine the concurrent rights to land of the Inca and the communities without recourse to this particular expression.

There is little doubt that many of the communities were pre-Incaic, and that their land arrangements were continued in Inca times. However, no one doubted that legally the Inca could move a whole community from one place to another if it were practical and expedient to do so.

In a symbolic way the Inca's theoretically absolute power probably did extend to universal ownership. If one assumes, as Inca culture apparently did, that the Inca could do anything he pleased with anyone or anything in the empire, one can easily conclude that the Inca enjoyed the rights of universal ownership. One should think of Inca universal ownership as a largely potential power running concurrently with customary local land rights.

Other characterizations are far more meaningful to the Inca legal structure than the application of the concept of title and usufruct. There were three principal types of land interest:

(1) that of working taxpayers which depended upon personal cultivation and tax service;

(2) that of the governing class which had cultivators supplied for the land;

(3) that of institutions, lands of the Inca and Sun perhaps to some extent overlapping (2).

Basic to the taxpayer's property interest and probably to most of the governing class, was the enduring connection of a family or families with particular lands through successive generations. For the taxpayers, their right to a share of community lands was dependent upon their membership in the community, upon their ability to work the land, and to do tax service. For the governing classes the right to hold lands and have them worked went with class and office. Institutional ownership carried tax-service rights that went parallel with the land interest.

These criss-crossing rights and duties and the points at which they interlock with political power provide the real basis of the Inca landholding system, while the conventional division of lands among Inca, Sun, and communities is a most inexact abstraction—little clarified by controversies over title and usufruct.

II · THE TAX SYSTEM

Some major outlines of the tax system are evident from the land organization. Food was the basic form of tribute or tax, since its accumulation underlay the financing of all other production and activities. To build a house or a palace, to fight a war, to mine metals, and to maintain craftsmen, stores had to be accumulated. Food and other maintenance supplies were not "pay" in any modern sense. They were gathered in storehouses to feed people while they were working. Analogies suggest themselves by the dozen among people of other cultures and more primitive organization: canoe building on the Northwest Coast and a Melanesian head hunt, for example, both involve the storing of food for a particular project. The Inca government did the same thing on a huge scale.

Not only did agricultural work and herding have to be done to finance government projects, but it also had to be done to maintain the administrators, the nobility, who did no manual labor. Thus the governing class as well as the government was financed by the effort of the agricultural communities.

Construction and war required man power. There was a labor draft to provide the men. The source of this man power was again the agricultural community whose men served on public projects in rotation.

The communal cultivation of Inca and Sun lands and the national side of the *mita* or labor service are generally the two aspects of the tax system emphasized. It is both the luck and the misfortune of subsequent writers on the Inca that Father Cobo organized his information exceedingly well, adhering to what were already in his time conventional attitudes to the

Inca material. His classifications have generally been taken as something inherent in the Inca system, in spite of his own statement that he is making an analogy to Spanish custom in what he classifies as tribute and what he does not.

It is commonly stated that in the Inca empire all taxes were paid in labor.[1] Cobo even says that everyone served the King personally;[2] by which one may assume that he meant that it was a non-feudal situation, that everyone served the Inca rather than being pledged to local nobility, which was in turn pledged to the Inca. This was far less true than one might surmise from Cobo's description. It is unfortunate that his inference in this respect has carried more force than the facts he cites. In the analysis of the tax system which follows, it will be evident that this system of centralized revenues produced by a submissive population, all at the command of the Inca, and principally for the imperial institutions—the Inca and Sun—is largely a construct of the chroniclers rather than a characteristic of Inca government.

To begin with, there is the matter of labor as the tax payment. In the case of food production on lands designated as belonging to the Inca or Sun, or herds so designated, Cobo and Polo and the other Spanish chroniclers saw the labor rather than the land produce as the tax paid. This was possibly because of their own orientation towards a money economy, or because such an interpretation was consistent with their legal theory that the Inca and Sun either held title to Inca and Sun land (and herds), or at least owned the usufruct. As the Inca could therefore hardly tax the land or produce that he already owned, they worked out the rationalization logically and said the only tax paid was the labor.

It is true, from the point of view of the agriculturalist or the herder, that what he gave was service. But from the standpoint of the Inca, governors, and *curacas*—what they received was produce. If one emphasizes services as the tax, an important distinction is lost between the cases in which a service is what is rendered and received, and the case in which service is rendered but goods are received.

It is no wonder that such an analysis should have appealed to adherents of the labor theory of value, and that the word "socialism" should have been pulled here and stretched there to fit the Inca. There is, in fact, nothing inherently wrong with looking at the Inca tax system in terms of labor service, provided that one is sufficiently interested in detail. It is important what labor was contributed to whom, and by whom required. But, it is also important what was produced and who spent it.

The tendency has been to neglect certain crucial points. Because Cobo confines the definition of "taxpayer" to agriculturalists, the work of persons who do not come within his classification has received less attention, as has the type of tribute which Cobo did not consider to be a tax. Yet craft production and the role of the craftsman tell a great deal about the Inca tax structure and system of government, as do the gifts given by the nobility to the Inca.

The tax system generally has been dealt with solely in terms of agricultural labor on the Inca and Sun lands and the *mita* service, stressing centralization of control and imperial projects. The taxes which went to provincial officials and the tax obligations of a purely local nature are rarely given their proper place. And as John Murra has said ". . . the welfare, socialist illusion is based not only on assigning to the state what was an *ayllu*, community function. It also comes from a misunderstanding of the redistributive role of the crown." [3]

It is conventional to give imperial taxation all the attention, while local taxation is all but ignored. The neglected information is in Cobo's writings and appears in the work of the other major chroniclers. Subsequent writers have tended to reiterate the material as originally organized, thus much that is important has remained obscure, however often repeated.

All able-bodied males over twenty-five—or younger, if married—shared community obligations. These agricultural producers are the only people whom Cobo counts as taxpayers.[4] All other occupations he counts outside the tax structure. The farmers held individual shares of community lands for their own use. The produce was not taxable, but the farmer's liability for agricultural tax labor and *mita* service went with the share of community lands. The basic agricultural tax consisted of communal labor in working the fields and keeping the flocks of the Inca, the Sun, and, though rarely mentioned, the governing officials. The community not only cultivated the *curaca's* fields,[5] but also had to build his house, keep his flocks,[6] and in general satisfy his economic needs. In addition it had to provide each administrator with one household servant per hundred taxpayers ruled.[7] These services which were rendered the *curacas* were not new in Inca times, but are said to have preceded Inca rule.[8] Community obligations also included maintaining local roads and bridges and such irrigation works as there were.[9]

The agriculturalists also were liable to do other *mita* service. The *mita* was of various sorts. There was the regular burden of providing the household service of *caciques*.[10] But it also could be a special call-up for work on national projects, such as building or war, and could involve service wherever the central government chose. The numbers available for draft were reported each year.[11] The agricultural communities worked (for his benefit) the share of community land of any member absent in army or *mita* service.[12] Cieza gives the impression that men were maintained by the province from which they came when working in Cuzco on a construction project of the "king."[13]

If this were so, the system of empire labor and agricultural taxation is seen divided completely into local segments. Instead of huge national storehouses in Cuzco accumulating supplies from the empire to be spent as the Inca emperor saw fit, each province sent men and their "mantenimiento." One would guess that the supplies came from provincial Inca storehouses. This seems absolutely consistent with the fact that De las Casas says that little food went to Cuzco from the Inca's stores.[14]

The communities also were obliged to weave cloth for the Inca and Sun,[15] probably for the *curacas*, and for themselves.[16] The amount of cloth to be made was fixed each year.[17] The wool they wove for themselves came from the community flocks; the wool for the Inca and the Sun came from their respective flocks. Polo [18] says that the weaving was done by the women, and by the sons until they married and placed themselves among the tribute payers. The references say that the weaving of clothing by the family for itself was a rigorously enforced obligation, as well as the other weaving taxes. Weaving of the special cloth of which the Inca emperor's garments were made was done continuously by the chosen women.[19] Weaving, then, though a tax obligation, was not done by persons whom Cobo counts as taxpayers.

Another duty of the communities which has some analogy to a tax, was the supplying of women for the houses of the chosen women. There was such a house in every province, run by an official, the *apopanaca*, who chose whatever girls under the age of 8 he thought suitably attractive. He was not held to any particular number. Annually, at the feast of Raymi, in February, the girls from the house who had reached 13 or 14 were brought to Cuzco. There they were distributed by the Inca or some representative of his. Some were made women of the Sun and put into service in various religious establishments. Some of these may ultimately have been used for sacrifice. Others of these young girls were given for the service of the Inca and for his wives and for relatives of his. They were given to such people as the Inca wished to reward or honor.[20] Males were also taken for sacrifice, but it is not clear how they were chosen.[21]

These tax obligations of the agricultural communities show a good deal about the government organization. The most striking characteristic is its extremely local nature. All tax-service was in terms of place of residence of the taxpayer, and most of it only could be performed locally. It is certainly important that man power was produced for national projects in geographical quotas. In the literature, the taxes of the empire government have been emphasized and the local tax burden neglected. It is no wonder that there were strictures on moving one's residence and that the permission of the *curaca* was required for travel. The system of rotation through which *mita* service was done, and the communal method of cultivating tax lands and meeting other village obligations required a fairly stable and fairly sedentary population.

The economic surplus was apparently sufficient to permit a draining off by the provincial and empire governments of some goods and man power, but it may not have been sufficient to allow much flexibility within the community once this was done. If a man's family needs him to farm their food, and if the community on which he depends socially and economically needs him to fulfill his share of group obligations, will he try to travel or move his home? Not unless leaving one place will provide him with a more advantageous situation in another.

In Inca times economic development was not such as to offer the farmer any livelihood away from his land. He was economically bound to it. The tax system brings to mind the feudal manor and the many variations of community agriculture found in other societies. Although the land-tenure system appears to have differed from the classic Inca pattern in some of the valleys of the pre-Inca Chimu kingdom, one can imagine how the same kind of taxes might have been extracted from agriculturalists in this area by the Inca government. In certain north coastal valleys, all the land was owned by the local *cacique*, and his tenants paid him a share of their produce.[22] No evidence has been found of how the taxes were applied, but it seems quite possible that lands were nevertheless allocated for the benefit of the Inca and Sun, and cultivated as a local communal obligation. The payments to the local lord could have gone on substantially as before. Throughout the empire, the Inca state probably tended to reinforce the community organization by increasing its common economic burden. The tax emphasis on community obligations, rather than on the cultivators as individuals, tightened what was probably a rather close community organization in the first place. Thus, while tying local communities to a larger whole, the Inca tax system also had an isolating and immobilizing effect.

THE SPECIALIST AND CRAFTSMAN AS NON-TAXPAYER
CRAFT PRODUCTS AS OFFICIAL GIFTS

Specialist and craft production (particularly of sumptuary articles) though not considered a basic tax, tells us much about the taxation system and property control under the Inca régime. There is strong evidence that the Inca provincial governor and the *curacas* were able to command and finance specialist and craft work. This confirms other indications of their favorable economic position and of their power, so much minimized by the "socialist-bureaucracy" theory of Inca government.

Cobo does not count as tribute the "rich presents" made to the Inca by the governors, captains, *caciques* and judges, because these gifts were voluntary, although he adds, they were customary.[23] The presents of the functionaries imply that these men were able to finance craftsmen and specialists. The latter were tax-exempt due to their specialization. Cobo designates mining, the crafts—including metal work, ceramics and weaving, and other skilled occupations—as substitutes for tribute.[24] Only agricultural laborers were counted as taxpayers, and only unskilled labor was tax-labor. Rowe gives Cobo's classification the stamp of approval by quoting it in full in his discussion of Inca taxation.[25]

Rowe [26] concludes that craftsmen manufactured only for the emperor, who distributed the surplus as gifts to the nobility. This goes too far in summarizing what took place. There was craft production for the *caciques* as well. How else could they have made "rich presents"? In the sources there is specific mention of craftsmen financed by and working for the Inca, the Sun, and the *caciques*.[27] Whether or not one regards the tribute-presents as a tax obligation of the *caciques* to the Inca, the duty of the craftsmen to the *caciques* was certainly very much like the tax-labor obligation of the agriculturalists.

The *caciques*, for reasons of sumptuary restriction, may not have used certain products for themselves directly, but instead used them to improve their positions by presenting them as gifts to higher government officials, or to the Inca. Even this is quite a different matter economically and politically from saying that craft production was exclusively for the Inca—let alone what may have been produced simply for the *caciques* themselves.

There is no doubt that gold and silver articles were one of the important gifts brought to the Inca, and that the Inca distributed these objects to the nobility as gifts. Santillán says they could be enjoyed only if given by the Inca.[28] Yet to state as Valera did,[29] that precious things like gold and silver, jewels, feathers, paints, copper, etc. could be had only by privilege and grace of the Inca is only to say that there were sumptuary laws.[30] The *Señores, curacas* and *orejones* were allowed ornaments proscribed to the ordinary man.[31] Are we to believe that these were all produced originally for the Inca?

Sumptuary laws do not mean that privileged persons received sumptuary goods exclusively from the Inca, but rather that they received the right to use them. Gifts were given, but in spite of Santillán, this does not necessarily mean that they were the only way to enjoy sumptuary privileges, nor the corollary proposed by Rowe, that all craft production was for the Inca.

Mining is a significant instance of how specialized work

fitted into the tax system. Cobo says that most gold and silver mining was financed and controlled by the local *caciques* who used the produce for gifts to the Inca.[32] The miners were local specialists; [33] their work therefore meant exemption from other tax-labor. This gives some intimation of the relation between local taxation and empire taxation, and of the power of the *curacas* over the lives of their subjects.

Miners were not the only specialists whose work meant exemption from the general work call-up. Weavers, metal workers, potters, stone workers—all were exempt from tax-labor other than in their crafts.[34] Their tools and raw materials were supplied them.

Some of the precious things given annually to the Inca were probably Inca financed, and simply presented by the *cacique*.[35] For example, Cobo specifically speaks of *cumbi* [36] cloth, which though worn by the nobility, could only be manufactured for the Inca who then distributed it as gifts. Cobo does not make this point about exclusive manufacture concerning the other things mentioned. Thus while some presented goods had been made for the Inca directly, others were the "rich presents" of the officials to the Inca. One has only to ask oneself how the *curacas* obtained these tribute or "gift" objects and how they obtained the labor to produce them, to surmise that the *curacas* had a type of tax power usually attributed solely to the Inca. They must have been able to command the services of craftsmen, and pay them, that is, maintain them and supply them with materials from local storehouses. These must either have been from their own stores, or they must have had discretion to draw on Inca and Sun storehouses. Probably both were true in various instances.

Working for the Inca or Sun probably often meant working for a provincial governor or shrine,[37] with only part of the craft production passed along to Cuzco. The rest was kept and used locally, either by reason of being granted to

an official by the Inca [38] or by being used in the local branch
of an imperial institution, such as a temple of the Sun.[39]

Thus, of all goods produced in the Inca's name, only a part
actually went to the Inca, while some remained for the very
government people who supervised the production. Cieza [40]
tells of many provincial silver workers, and of articles of gold
and silver belonging to the Inca which remained in the provincial capitals, while in Cuzco there were craftsmen working
these metals directly for the Inca.[41]

One can take the view that all skilled workers were like
taxpayers in their craft obligations. This would certainly be
the role of those who were simultaneously members of an
agricultural community, having a share of community land.
Specialists such as miners, who worked as such only a few
months of the year probably fit into this category. But what
of goldsmiths, and silversmiths, and other craftsmen? Did
they work at their crafts to the exclusion of all agricultural
work? Some of the sources seem to imply that they did. In
this case we must recognize some similarities between these
craftsmen in the Inca empire and the skilled slave elsewhere.
Fed, clothed, and maintained by his "employer," the craftsman was obliged to ply his craft for life—his tools and materials being supplied. The comparable unskilled class were the
yanaconas who were attached to a particular master for life
and who apparently did agricultural work.[42] Both craftsmen
and *yanaconas* served only the Inca and the nobility. Both
served for life. Both were maintained completely.

One sees in these various fragments of information about
specialized and craft production that it is probably going too
far to say that all craft work was for the emperor. This magnifies
the already well-established myth of complete central control.
Cacique is a vague term. One does not know how far down
the administrative hierarchy there was economic ability to
support full-time craftsmen, or even to finance them part time.

But it is likely that all craft work was not for the Inca—that even a large part of what actually was produced for him was only nominally so.

This points to stratification of power, which grand statements such as Cobo's that "everyone served the Inca personally" tend to obscure. Like the evidence of *curaca* land interests, the ability to command craft production suggests that the tyrannical role of local officials, so much deplored after the Conquest, probably was not without its roots in Inca and pre-Inca political structure.

HOW THE PIE WAS SLICED

The spending of the agricultural tax produce was governed fundamentally by the rule that if a man worked for someone, the "employer" was obliged to feed, clothe, and supply him with working materials during the period of his employment.[43] This applied to tax-labor as well as non-tax-labor, such as craft work. The "employer" might be the government, the Sun, or some particular official. Needless to say, only the government, religious institutions, or officials, had the resources to employ labor, or the right to do so through the *mita* system. However, work may have been exchanged by the Indians among themselves in the *aine* system.[44]

One usually thinks of Inca taxes, both in goods and labor, as being spent on the great construction projects and wars for which the Inca are famous. But for the immediate purpose it is more illuminating to look closely at the normal tax burden, rather than to confine oneself to these more striking special projects.

In postulating a bureaucracy in which all government officials are supported by tax-stores, it is important to realize how food stores were accumulated and spent. The fact that many persons were supported by the tax system has been exaggerated to transform Inca society into a complete bureaucracy. The usual list of persons who were tax-exempt includes: [45]

(1) all persons of Inca blood;

(2) all administrative officials in the decimal hierarchy down to and including the centurions (and probably at least at some levels their sons and grandsons);

(3) minor officials during the period of office;

(4) the chosen women (though they wove cloth and performed other duties which are not counted);

(5) religious functionaries connected with the Sun cult;

(6) specialists and craftsmen (though they were obliged to work in their specialties);

(7) men over 50, and men under 25 if unmarried;

(8) all persons who were unable to work because of illness or incapacity;

(9) women (though they had to weave tax cloth [46] and girls were liable to become chosen women).

In some instances, of course, the performance of one tax service exempted the individual from the performance of another. For example, a man doing army service was exempt from doing his share of work on Inca and Sun fields.

Also exempt from taxes were the *yanaconas*.[47] They appear to have been much like slaves—lifetime retainers who served the Inca and tilled his fields in the Cuzco region.[48] Castro and Ortega Morejón [49] say that the Inca gave *yanaconas* to *curacas* of *guarangas* and *pachacas,* and that they were ordinary taxpayer Indians. Santillán [50] says the same. Bandera [51] relates that they were all the sons of *señores,* not in the charge of the *curacas,* but solely of the governors, and that they were concerned with the cultivation of the fields of the Inca.

A list of the tax-exempt shows how limited was Cobo's definition of the taxpayer. There are many persons who performed obligatory services outside the tax system, and who did not contribute to the reserve of agricultural produce. The relations between these groups were complex. For example, the list of the tax-exempt includes the nobility who constituted the "employers," and tax-exempt craftsmen and specialists, some of whom they employed. The shares of tax produce which these two groups received differed widely. The one spent the tax produce to, among other things, support the other. The economic interlocking which this implies gives an intimation of the social realities which the list omits.

A review of the list of tax-exempt persons with its mélange of aristocrats, administrators, priests, craftsmen, and dependent persons (women, under or over aged persons, and the sick) shows it to be less a list of the idle than one might first suppose. Some of the persons on the list (craftsmen, women, the young), though not counted as taxpayers were engaged in obligatory productive work, while others were much more in the way of being clean-handed aristocrats. Some did not do tax-work because of incapacity (the aged and sick), but others simply because of class or caste (those of Inca blood, and administrators).

Cobo would have us believe that the job of tax collecting and governing was so arduous that for persons of noble breed it was altogether equivalent to tax-labor. Must one be very cynical to see Cobo's conception as a personal justification of a blood aristocracy in which he firmly believed?

A consideration of tax spending from a geographic point of view indicates the close connection between this and local tax production. Storehouses of the Inca and Sun—nominally completely imperial institutions—were found in three places: locally near the fields, in each provincial capital, and in Cuzco. All were places of consumption as well as of production.

The kind of tax-labor which filled these storehouses was done for the *curaca* and for the good of the community, as well as for the Inca and other national institutions. Thus many of the Inca taxes were analogous to local taxes. There were labor obligations on the national level which also (and probably previously) existed on the community level. These range from the repair of roads to the service of officials.

The communities were responsible for the maintenance of

local roads, bridges, and irrigation works, the service of local shrines, and the provision of household service for *curacas*. The tax burdens for the construction and maintenance of imperial roads probably differed little from those assessed for local roads. The two road systems differed principally in that the one was centrally planned, running the length of the empire, having at regular intervals *tambos* and post runners, while the other served local purposes. Support for the construction and maintenance of both road systems came from local labor, locally supplied with food and tools.[52]

According to the principle that tax-labor was supported by the "employer," *mita* labor working on the Inca royal roads must have been cared for by tax produce from local Inca storehouses. How were men supported when they worked on the maintenance of other roads? Did they provide their own food and tools? Possibly. Or perhaps community labor in maintaining local roads was also supported from the Inca storehouses, since produce from community lands went to individual families, and not to a community storehouse. One is repeatedly told by the chroniclers that produce from community lands was never taxed in any way. The "employer" had the obligation to maintain labor. Who was the "employer" in the case of local roads? The only tax-stores available for such a purpose would seem to be the Inca stores. Be that as it may, many local roads were undoubtedly pre-Incaic and it is probable that their construction and maintenance was a pre-Incaic community obligation. The building and the repairing of Inca royal roads are seen in the context of pre-Inca local roads, not solely in the ways in which they were an imperial innovation.

The imperial government itself must be seen taxwise in terms of its local segments. Not only were the provincial capitals centers of tax collection; they were also centers of tax expenditure.

Each provincial capital had palaces, a fortress, a temple of the Sun, a house of chosen women, and the most important storehouses in the district. The latter were used to support officials, "servants of the Inca," the military who might pass there, a royal *tambo,* and many Indians of the neighboring towns who were doing their *mita* service.[53] This probably was all locally financed. De las Casas [54] tells us that little food went to Cuzco from the Inca's stores, and Cobo [55] indicates that the governors had a good deal of discretion over the expenditure of the Inca's tax stores.

Some taxes harvested for the Inca were not even taken to the provincial capital, but remained in local storehouses, among other purposes for the provisioning of *tambos* which were one day's journey apart; for the feeding of armies which might pass through, or for royal parties or emissaries.[56] The poor, namely those members of the community too old or ill to do agricultural labor, also were supported in part by the Inca storehouses, as was the whole local population in a year of famine.[57] These local stores were also [58] used to maintain the agriculturalists when they served in local segments of provincial or national projects, such as the building and repairing of storehouses, roads, and irrigation works near their own communities.[59]

For the analogous use in the provinces of the Sun lands,[60] one has only to be reminded of the numerous local *huacas* (idols or shrines) and their attendants, and of the temple of the Sun in the provincial capital on which part of these stores were spent.

While the Cuzco court, at least in part, depended on the empire for support, the sources give the distinct impression that the provinces were economically interdependent only to a slight degree even in the expenditure of tax-stores. Specialized local products were traded by those in charge, from the storehouses of the valleys to the highlands and vice versa. In times of great need in one area, stores of a more fortunate province could be tapped.[61]

It is clear enough that neither agricultural tax produce, nor the performance of *mita* service was expended principally on a national level. Quite the contrary, the largest part of both appears to have been expended within the locality or the area of the province. The institutions in the provincial capital were segments of an imperial structure, to be sure, and some produce, some man power, and some women were sent to Cuzco, which could call for these in what quantities it chose. But choice was limited by regard for normal local expenditure.

The normal economic task of serving and supporting the local governing classes seems to have been a proportionately large part of the tax burden. One can estimate the number of administrators who did not do manual labor in a province by taking the theoretical structure of the decimal system as a basis. While the decimal system is undoubtedly a highly approximate abstraction, some gross conclusions can be derived from it. Of a taxpayer population of 40,000 (a province), there were 400 rulers of 100 entitled to one servant each; 80 rulers of 500 entitled to 5 servants each; 40 rulers of 1,000 entitled to 10 servants each; four rulers of 10,000 [62] entitled to 100 manservants each; and the governor himself, entitled to 400. Thus 2,000 men were engaged in the basic *mita* household service of the provincial officials while their fields were worked by the communities.[63] Of these only 400 served an Inca official. The remaining 1,600 served the *curacas*. These men all had families and when they were absent in *mita* service their shares of communal lands were worked by the community from which they came. Five percent of the able-bodied man power was—in theory at least—occupied in *mita* service within the province, mostly in the service of the *curacas*.[64] In short, 2,000 *mita* workers were 5 percent of the total taxpayer population (40,000) of a province.

To see this basic *mita* tax in proportion to imperial taxation, one may consider the number of men required for the largest construction project of the Inca at Sachsahuaman. This has been said to have involved 30,000 men at one time. The total number of men involved in the provincial *mita* service at any time was probably more than twice as large.

This figure is arrived at in the following way. The population of the Andean area in Inca times has been estimated at 8,000,000.[65] Assuming a family to consist of five persons with only one taxpayer, each province of 40,000 taxpayers had an approximate population of 200,000. Thus there were about 40 provinces.[66] The 30,000 men who were needed for Sachsahuaman were called up from an eligible taxpayer population of about 1,600,000, that is, they constituted about 1.9 percent of the taxpayer population. In all probability the most gigantic national project called up fewer than half the number of men who were regularly engaged in provincial personal *mita* service of officials—let alone other provincial *mita* projects.

Taking a much lower population estimate for the Andean area, let us say 4,000,000, while keeping the same figure for the construction of Sachsahuaman, namely 30,000 men, the results are still fairly heavily on the side of local *mita* service. In that case 3.8 percent of the taxpayer population would be required to build Sachsahuaman, while 5 percent were regularly engaged in provincial *mita* service.

What food stores would have been necessary to finance the building of Sachsahuaman? If the population was 8,000,000, the size of the Inca lands throughout the empire need not have constituted more than 2 percent of the size of community lands to have supported the 30,000 men. This is even without considering the practice of accumulating tax-stores over a period of years, which would have permitted the percentage to be much lower. In fact, Inca tax-stores were used for many local and provincial purposes at the same time that they were used to finance imperial projects. Hence the tax-lands were probably larger than the minimum size required to build Sachsahuaman. Since the percentage of Inca and Sun lands could be quite low indeed and still support great numbers of men for national works, there is no reason to suppose that the principal tax burden was for imperial purposes. By no extension of this evidence should one find it necessary to say that Inca lands constituted one-third of the land.[67]

The same general conclusions apply also to the Sun lands and to the national religion in general. Cobo and Polo tell us that Sun storehouses were everywhere smaller than Inca storehouses.[68] Further we know of considerable diversion of Sun produce to support local shrines and deities. As for the houses of the chosen women, they were probably not a very large economic burden. Cieza, who is not given to modest numerical estimates, speaks for example, of a temple of the Sun in which there were all of 200 beautiful maidens.[69]

The basic decimal figures used here are often cited and are generally accepted as approximate, but they are not applied to the tax system. The result of their application is to place imperial taxation in some context with local taxation. The figures used for these calculations are all so arguable that one can come only to the grossest conclusions. But it seems worth following them through if only to discover that whether one uses a high population estimate or a low one, the normal burden of local tax-labor engaged in the personal service of officials alone remained heavier than the national Inca draft for its largest project. Assuming one gives any credence at all to the decimal system, it is worth seeing what it implies. This evidence simply confirms the evidence seen earlier [70] on the relative extent of Inca, *curaca,* and community lands. Material cited earlier on the Chincha Valley also indicates that local Inca tax-lands were somewhat smaller than *curaca* lands.

It is not intended to minimize the amount of organization involved in the tax system, nor to assume that the burden on the agricultural taxpayer was necessarily light. But in view of the simplified way in which the land tax system is described by most writers from the chroniclers to the present day, and the general disregard of certain implications of the information given, it becomes necessary to insist on those details which show a more probable picture. The same applies to the man power draft. It was a remarkable achievement. Of that there is no doubt. However, that is no reason to be so awed by the organizational achievement as to forget what the tax system might have meant in terms of food storage and labor obligations. The *mita* service was local as well as national. The numbers of persons involved in one of the largest building projects undertaken was much smaller than the number regularly employed in local *mita* service. The conventional distortion of the tax system is consistent with a general overestimate of the magnitude of imperial government.

THE POWER TO TAX

The Inca and His Councilors. Tax demands to the localities were presented by the Inca and his councilors. These demands were based upon census and storehouse figures collected annually,[71] and were arrived at after consultation among the Inca, his council and governors.[72]

One may reasonably assume that the size of Inca and Sun lands was usually fixed on conquest of a province. Revenues from these lands must have been limited by their size. The discretion exercised by the Inca and his councilors was consequently not over the amount of food to be produced for them, but over the amount to be removed from the local and provincial storehouses to whatever place they designated. Care was always taken to leave the province taken care of for ordinary expenditures.[73] Cobo and Polo say that the only measure of the tax was the will of the Inca.[74] Yet Polo mentions the quantity of agricultural produce in terms of what the land yielded and [75] of the quantity of rich presents to the Inca, that is, of craft products and precious metals, depending upon the generosity of either the provincial governor or the

curaca, and the industriousness of the local *mamaconas,* craftsmen, and general population.[76] The number of women brought
to Cuzco seems to have depended on how many happened
to be of suitable age at the time of the feast of Raymi in each
house of chosen women. The number in the house is said to
have been governed by the discretion of the Apopanaca.[77]

Theoretically, the number of men to be called up for a
national project was entirely within the central government's
discretion.[78] It was determined by the Inca and his governors.
But here again there was the limitation of economic fact.
Only as many men could be called as could be fed, clothed,
and supplied with work materials.[79] Some consideration was
also given lest the ordinary affairs of the province be unneces-
sarily disrupted. Cieza gives the distinct impression that when
men were sent to Cuzco to work on construction projects of
the king they were maintained by the province which sent
them.[80]

Tax demands made by the Inca and his councilors, either in
terms of stores, or men called up, were announced to the
"caciques, curacas y capitanes" assembled in Cuzco.[81] To
read the accounts, after being wined and dined they were
happy to comply with what was demanded of them. One may
well have doubts about this since the enforcement of tax requirements had such a prominent place in the Inca governing
machinery. The provincial governors (and other high officials?)
divided the assigned tasks among themselves and in turn
shifted the burden equitably among subordinates in the administrative hierarchy, and so on down the line until the taxpayer himself was reached. Efforts were made to keep the
burden from falling more heavily on one community than
another, and demands which could be distributed equally or
borne in turn were dealt with this way. This obviously was not
the case where a region specialized in some particular product
or service, but applied only to the unspecialized agricultural
community.[82] Every community contributed something, and

the production of taxable articles was started where it did not exist on conquest.[83] Cieza describes the taxes [84] as if the allocation might have differed from province to province, not only in special items but also in basic type of assessment. Other chroniclers like Cobo, tend to emphasize equality of tax assessment.

One gets the impression that apart from maintaining the splendor of the court—for which tax requirements must have been fairly regular—special tax demands of the Cuzco government were made principally for two purposes, for war, or for building projects. These were the two major undertakings decided on the imperial level.[85]

The Inca Governor and the Curacas. As we now know, the same types of taxes were paid to the *curacas* and governors as were paid to the central government. Their houses were built, their fields cultivated, their flocks tended, and each had *mita* workers at his disposal. They could command the service of craftsmen, and they supervised the production of sumptuary articles. This production was not all directly for themselves, but indirectly so, in that they could not enjoy the use of such sumptuary articles as *cumbi* cloth until it had been given them by the Inca. They gave the Inca certain sumptuary goods produced in their province and the Inca gave them presents in return.

While the same types of taxes which were paid to the central government were paid to the provincial governors and the *curacas,* these officials did not have great discretion over how much was to be paid. One gathers that there was a top limit fixed. The number of *mita* workers, for example, was limited to one per hundred taxpayers governed. The Inca governor had discretion over the expenditure of some of the Inca and Sun stores. But the *curacas* probably had limited access to such resources.

Local building and road projects were financed locally, though done in the name of the Inca and Sun. Even the maintenance of *mita* workers serving in Cuzco on a national project seems to have been financed by the province from which they were sent.[86]

All the man power and tax surplus drained off by the central government might, in pre-Inca times, have been spent locally. The greater magnificence of pre-Inca Huamachuco compared with the Inca city may be evidence of this.[87] But another important consideration is the jealous guarding of power and sumptuary symbols on the part of the central government. While local rulers were not removed when conquered, and while they were not stripped of their property, neither did they enjoy their previous governing powers. They could not exploit the local population for their own ends beyond a fixed point. But it is unnecessary to assume that this was entirely a question of central government benevolence, of Inca wisdom in protecting the populace from its governors and *curacas*. Far more probably, there was a great concern lest there be rebellion against the central government or competition with it for resources. Even the Inca governors, who must have formed a relatively trusted inner circle, were spied on, checked on, and limited by law to dependence on the Inca for some sumptuary articles. This fear of local strength suggests that a good deal of local power and loyalty remained in the conquered kingdoms.

One can only guess at how much the governors bargained with the central government, and the *curacas* with the governors for local, as against national, exploitation and expenditures. One can also guess that it was through depriving them of some independent taxing rights that defeated local rulers were in fact stripped of power while they continued in office. From the point of view of the taxpayer, the *curaca's* power would not have been appreciably altered. For example, in pre-Inca times the ruler of a province had the right to raise an army for a war he chose to wage; under the Inca yoke, he lost this right and discretion. In its place he had the obligation to draft men for an army when the Cuzco government or the provincial governor demanded it. The taxpayer's obligations remained the same, and the official who made the direct demand on him was not changed. However, the source of the discretionary decision was changed. The taxpayer would have continued to have the same labor obligations as previously, perhaps even more, and the *curaca* would still be the official enforcing his performance of duty. While some of it was directly for the *curaca's* benefit, some of it was to meet tax demands from higher up in the administrative hierarchy. This itself, except for the highest ranking *curacas*, was probably a pre-Inca relationship in the more developed valleys of the empire.

It was the *curaca's* responsibility to produce the tax goods or the tax-labor demanded of his sector. He, rather than any balky taxpayers, was liable for any failure. A good example is the punishment of the *curaca* for failure to maintain a *tambo* properly. The maintenance of these resting places was a local tax duty. If anything was missing in a *tambo*, the *curaca* in charge was chastised. He passed along the punishment by forcing his pueblo to make good the loss and inflicting penalty on the culprit.[88] This is an illustration of the relation between governing and governed. The governing official was personally responsible for the fulfillment of duty by those under his supervision. He had a stake in the exploitation of the people under him, even when the service or goods were not for him. And while the *curacas* may not have had discretion over the quantity of the tax and how it was to be spent—a choice the higher ranking of them probably enjoyed in pre-Inca days—they retained a very considerable power over the taxpayers. The lower ranking *curacas* had the final say about who was to do what *mita* service, and who was to have what share of community lands; they had the independent power to punish, short of the death penalty, and with permission from above, even the power to impose the death penalty itself.

It is all very well to speak as the chroniclers do of rotation of *mita* service, of annual reallocation of community lands, and of equal distribution of the tax burden, as if these were by reason of their mechanism bound to be just. But there were more and less desirable *mita* duties, and more and less desirable shares of community land. The *curacas* as well had discretion over some of the distribution from Inca and Sun storehouses in times of need and in times of surplus. The personal wealth of the *curaca* depended in some measure on how much work he could get out of the people from whom he had the right to exact labor. So did his status *vis à vis* the central government. For example, the more cloth and sumptuary goods he could get them to produce, the better his position as a giver of gifts to the mighty. There was severe punishment and an increase in taxes assessed for any tax cheating.[89]

Because he deplored Spanish exploitation, Polo presented a description of Inca officialdom as a benevolent hierarchy of paternalistic tax collectors. He felt that with the Inca government decapitated, and the limitations on the *curacas* removed, all benevolence went out the window and the *curacas* became ruthless exploiters. It seems plausible that in Spanish times the *curacas* had the freedom to go to extremes that might not have been possible under the Inca government. But the contrast in behavior in pre-Inca and post-Inca times has been overdrawn. Putting the whole together: a tax structure in which officials were liable for taxes produced by those they governed; the absence of any possible appeal by the taxpayer for whom the *curaca's* decision on any matter was final; the economic dependence of the official on the work of his subjects; all these suggest that *curaca* power and *curaca* petty tyrannies existed long before Spanish times.[90]

What has been said of the *curaca's* position in the tax system, *vis à vis* the central government and the taxpayer, probably applies in a large measure to the Inca provincial governor himself, in his relations with the Cuzco government. He was in a position in which the more he could bring from his province to Cuzco, or turn for his own profit, the better.

The central government, in draining off a certain amount for itself, and in limiting the extent to which officials from the governor down could use their positions for personal aggrandizement, put outside curbs on local taxing power, but they far from eliminated local taxation. The tax position of the *curacas* and also of the provincial governor show concretely the structure of the imperial government. One cannot, after examining the tax system, think of Inca government in terms of a paternalistic empire of almost utopian plan. The interlocking of local and national interests has a contemporary (one might even say a universal) flavor of competition for resources and power. One can see the power of local rulers as diminished by Inca defeat in their loss of ultimate discretion, but one can also see them more securely entrenched in their ruling positions because the crushing power of a larger government backed them up, insuring their positions against the insecurities of rebellion and war. The governors and *curacas* enforced the Inca's rule, his taxes and laws, but they did not neglect to fill their own larders at the same time. This exploitation by officials for themselves was as much a part of the system as was their job in producing what Cuzco demanded. The conception of a selfless, salaried bureaucracy melts away on close inspection of the actual economic arrangements.

III · SOME FURTHER RULES OF SUBSTANTIVE LAW

CRIMINAL LAW, AND
COMPENSATION FOR DAMAGE OR INJURY

Lists of crimes and their penalties are not infrequent in the accounts of the chroniclers.[1] An extensive sample of these is included in the Appendix. These lists are very crude and not entirely consistent with one another. A simple statement that the penalty for killing was death is almost hopelessly incomplete for scholarly purposes. Yet most of the source material is no more explicit than this. There are no cases. Little or nothing is said of local variation.

Not only are the statements about crime too condensed to be very meaningful, but undoubtedly much has not even been mentioned. What rapid answer would one elicit by asking "What is a crime in the United States?" Murder and robbery? Would anyone say "adultery, incest, sodomy?" Would anyone remember that it is a misdemeanor to spit on the floor of the subway? Yet this and thousands of other rules are common knowledge. Would anyone think to mention a situation in which a homicide is not a murder? Who would be able to describe the complex of interrelationships which are fundamental to any conception of theft? Consider the intricate cultural assumptions involved in the operation of so common an institution as a public library.

The frustrating incompleteness of the chroniclers' lists is sadly obvious, both as to content and coverage. Yet in dealing with them in two lengthy scholarly studies,[2] Hermann Trimborn has succumbed to the temptation of treating the bits and pieces as if they were some sort of reliable formal codification, unwritten, yet a systematic whole. Apart from his singular emphasis on the study of punishments, he is preoccupied with such questions as whether the Inca criminal law evidences an objectivist, or subjectivist mentality. He makes subtle distinctions among types of double crimes, combined rape-incest, or murder-robbery, for example, from which he extracts principles of punishment. In short, he occupies himself with the theory of a criminal law of which the facts are barely known. In the course of his meticulous compilation, he extracts from the Spaniards' poor bare statements of general rules, some refined distinctions of his own manufacture. He superimposes on the material his own conception of the evolution of law and legal theory. Yet his compilation of material is of great interest, however one may differ with aspects of his analysis.

Rather than accord Spanish statements of Inca rules the subtle analysis reserved for statutes and holy books, for present purposes it is useful to look at crude stuff crudely, looking for the large distinctions and the striking ones.

Striking, though certainly not unique to the Inca, was the privilege granted to the ruler and in part to the ruling class to commit certain crimes, or rather acts which were crimes if committed by a commoner. Leaving out sumptuary laws entirely, and turning to certain of the major offenses which could carry the capital penalty—incest, homicide and theft—a most interesting phenomenon is seen. The Inca emperor was permitted all three in certain forms. The Inca could commit incest with his sister, who was also his principal wife. The Inca and his governors could apply the death penalty as they saw fit, that is, they could commit a legal homicide. One may wonder what limitations of process there were on this privilege, if any. The Inca could confiscate the property of those who were considered to have committed a crime against him,[3] and could in some, if not in all cases, apply the property to his own use.[4]

The Inca could, in short, with certain limitations, commit a legal theft.

The nobility, though it did not enjoy all of these special privileges of the Inca emperor, had considerably more than the commoners. Any illegal act committed by a noble invariably carried a lesser penalty than the same act committed by a commoner.[5] Incest, which carried the death penalty for commoners, involved merely a public reprimand for the nobility. Acosta, in fact, says that both the Inca and the nobles could marry their sisters.[6] Some writers are reluctant to take this statement at face value, and insist that Acosta must have meant classificatory sisters rather than siblings. Either way, the sexual privilege was considerable.

The use of state power to shield the rulers of the state from certain criminal penalties, or to soften these penalties is an extremely significant one. It gives the lie to the conception of the noble noble, of the purer morality of the nobility. It suggests that the nobility, as enforcer of the law, was moved by a singularly convenient double standard. Rather than regard the exemption of the noble from common penalties as the emblem of the ethically high-minded, one could say that it was simply the privilege of the powerful. Just as it was easier for a Greek aristocrat equipped with a chariot and horses to be more heroic at war than a foot soldier accompanying him, so was it possible for the Inca nobility to be more moral than the commoners who could not cloak their anti-social acts with legal privilege. With what delicacy of feeling did the Inca (or Cobo for them) rationalize this differentiation by saying that to an Inca of royal blood, public reprimand meant as much as the death penalty to a commoner.[7]

Writers on the Inca have said that the criminal law was severe. Rowe, Cunow, Trimborn, Baudin—all make this sober comment.[8] Severity is a comparative term. But with whom are the Inca being compared? The impression of severity probably is given by these characteristics: the Inca rigorously punished certain acts that we do not punish, or punish only lightly; Inca punishments were usually physical, neither fines, imprisonment, nor slavery were generally used; and probably most impressive is the fact that for their own peculiar reasons the chroniclers saw fit to mention the death penalty more frequently than any other, and sometimes as if it applied to virtually all offences.[9] Yet even in serious cases, in describing judicial practice,[10] the judges are said not to have applied a fixed punishment, but to have sentenced for crimes as they saw fit.[11] One cannot know how discretion was actually exercised. Furthermore, it is clear from even a cursory look at the administrative system, that most minor criminal matters must have been handled summarily by the local administrative officials who did not have the independent power to condemn to death, but of these matters the record is almost blank. Local officials may have punished in any number of ways, not only with the lesser physical penalties which are usually mentioned. They could surely give preferential treatment to favored persons in the distribution of tax-labor tasks—as in the distribution of fields for cultivation. Perhaps they were even able to exact compensatory labor or the payment of stored food or other property for minor offenses. There are hints of this in the instances in which compensation for economic damage is involved. However, if these economic penalties existed at all, and there is no certainty of it, they in no way involved the standardization, nor the breadth of application that was common-place in Aztec Mexico.

That Inca punitive methods ordinarily did not include fines, nor most forms of slavery, nor our type of imprisonment, but consisted largely of physical punishments [12] is closely related to Inca economic development. The Aztecs regularly used fines and slavery and it suited their economic system. In the Andean culture area, fines and slavery were less practical. To pay a fine a man must either own something he can pay with or have a means of acquiring it. For the Inca taxpayer, the opportunity to accumulate property was very limited. As for slavery, the Inca agriculturalist would not have had the means either of supporting or exploiting a slave, while government officials had an ample supply of labor through the tax system for personal service, as well as for government projects. Slave labor as a punishment for crime does appear to have been used on the Inca's coca plantations,[13] but this would seem to be a special instance. That physical punishment commonly was used in the penal system seems attributable at least in part to economic conditions, rather than solely to temperamental severity.

Polo [14] tells us that *except for the nobles,* the Indians were unconcerned with accumulating personal property. Unconcerned or unable to—this, rather than an elaborate Garcilasan rationalization [15] about justice and ridding the republic of wrongdoers, is probably a basic reason why there were not more economic penalties. Garcilaso evidently thought that the severe penalties resulted in there being "hardly a delict to be punished from one end of the year to the next in the whole empire of the Inca." [16] This is most unlikely. It is hard to imagine how Garcilaso could have known such a thing. It sounds like one of his complimentary inventions to praise the Inca. One cannot, for example, infer that because armies passing through the countryside were forbidden to take anything from the places they crossed, under threat of severe punishment, that they took nothing. Any experience with any army would suggest otherwise. The severity of a penalty may indicate a strong wish to deter. But the threat by itself does not mean that there were no violations. It rather suggests the opposite.

There were no court fees [17] so there was no motive for the government to encourage private litigation. Nevertheless there appear to have been certain tort-like situations as well as some crimes in which compensation for economic damage seems to have had a part in determining the penalty. There is some slight evidence that restitution and repayment may have had some role in compensating the victim of a theft.[18] However, punishment involving no economic aspect is more commonly mentioned. Some exceptions follow: Cobo [19] tells us that if any flocks damaged neighboring fields, the owner of the fields had the right to take animals to the extent of the damage done. One who injured another in such a way that he could no longer work at ordinary tasks, was obliged to support the injured man in addition to sustaining punishment for having caused injury.[20] If he had no estate out of which to support his victim, the Inca fed him out of his estate, and the wrongdoer's punishment was augmented. One who burned down a house was put to death, but he also had to pay for the damage out of his property.[21] If he burned down his own house out of negligence and the house of another burned down in consequence, he was obligated to make good the damage.[22] In spite of the fact that these are instances of economic penalties, they tend to confirm the impression that such penalties were the exception rather than the rule. In the instance of livestock doing damage, the existence of a source of compensation is identical with the cause of the damage. In the case of personal injury the possibility that there were no resources from which to support the victim is recognized by the rule itself. In the burning of a house, rebuilding principally involved the contribution of labor. Labor might also be the principal means of supporting an injured man. The payment of goods is involved with certainty only in the livestock damage.

The law of homicide is a good example of the type of material Inca criminal law presents, both in form and content. It touches on a wide range of Inca life.

Crudity of presentation is epitomized by Poma de Ayala's and De las Casas' simple statements that persons who killed someone without justification were themselves killed.[23] Happily other accounts are somewhat more detailed.

Adultery was a justification for homicide in circumstances which will be enumerated. This is an instance of allowing a private individual to enforce the law. It differs from the modern "crime of passion" in which, in some jurisdictions, adultery excuses or mitigates the penalties on homicide. In these modern situations adultery does not itself carry the death penalty. Inca law places this sexual act on a level with the most serious offenses, and permits private enforcement.

An Indian who killed his wife for adultery went free. If he killed her for some other offense his punishment depended on his rank. If he were an ordinary taxpayer, he was condemned to death. If he were of high rank, the Inca punished him in some way short of death. A woman who killed her husband was hanged by the feet until she was dead.[24]

Valera enumerates many homicides, all of them carrying the death penalty in some form, except for the case of the husband who kills an adulterous wife[25] or her lover.[26] There seems to have been no justifiable homicide of a husband by a wife, although a husband was justified in killing his wife for adultery, showing the great disparity between the sexes in permissible behavior. Wide distinction in status between men and women is seen throughout Inca law, and the criminal law iterates it in yet another context. The rules with respect to the killing of an adultress make it clear that the law was not the same for all persons, either as between men and women or as between commoners and persons of rank. Cobo, in fact, simply states that all crimes were penalized differently according to the rank of the defendant.[27]

In contrast to adultery is the law referring to official use of the death penalty. The *t'oqrikoq* was the lowest official with the right to impose this punishment independently. An official of lower rank who killed one of his Indian subjects without Inca permission was publicly punished by being beaten with a stone for the first offense and killed for the second. But if out of grace he were spared the death penalty, he was removed from office and exiled.[28] Thus, the central government jealously reserved for itself the exclusive right to punish homicide. Neither the *ayllu* nor family of the murdered man, had any right to take the law into its own hands. The immediate governing official had to obtain permission from above. The central government alone had the authority to act independently.[29]

This is an extremely important indicator of the development of Inca government. One has only to compare it with more primitive arrangements where self-help, clan feuds, and retaliatory killings are the order of the day to realize what the state had become by Inca times. Some writers have overstressed the kin units as mosaic bits of the empire, equivalent to the decimal units, thereby obscuring the fact that these kin groups were not the same functioning government bodies they are in cultures where there is no state. The units may be the same quantitatively, but their function is changed. And the Inca law of homicide makes this emphatically clear. The state not only reserved to itself exclusively the punishment of homicide, but it also allowed its officials the privilege of being somewhat less vulnerable to the law than the common taxpayer. Even an illegal homicide by an official was not punished with the severity reserved for killers without official rank. Was there any limitation on the Inca himself? The tone of the sources suggests that the Inca could order an execution at his pleasure.

One who killed another in order to rob was imprisoned for many days of torture and then killed.[30] The penalty for homicide in the course of a quarrel depended on who was the' instigator. If the dead man began the fight, the killer was exiled to the tropical coca plantations of the Inca; but if the killer had caused the quarrel, he was put to death. He who killed treacherously was condemned to death whatever his rank.[31]

Homicide by witchcraft resulted in death, not only of the killer, but of his whole family. This may be a remnant of some former family responsibility for the actions of its members. But we are told that the rule was in order that no one should survive who knew witchcraft.[32] It is evident from the accounts that not only the Inca believed in witchcraft, but that their Spanish chroniclers also did.

Omitted from most accounts of homicide under Inca law, but found in the sources in connection with religion is human sacrifice and retainer burial. Denied by some [33] and asserted by others,[34] one cannot but concur with Rowe [35] in the fact that human sacrifice did exist. The punishment of murder by witchcraft and human sacrifice as a sanctioned form of homicide both show the more primitive side of Inca development.

The law of homicide taken as a whole helps to place the Inca political system in a concrete position relative to other cultures. It sharply curbs the temptation to discuss state achievements without mentioning the primitive milieu in which the state functioned.

Another primitive aspect of the Inca attitude toward crime was the belief that all physical illness, deformity, or other misfortune was a form of supernatural punishment for crime or failure to perform religious duties. Like most believers in divine justice, however, the Inca placed no reliance on the supernatural to carry out all punishments. Ample human assistance was usually provided. Some form of confession seems to have been a native institution.[36] It is not clear whether the confession of crime for religious purposes ever resulted in secular punishment. Molina and Murúa say that confession was secret, though the latter does assert that there were some exceptions. There does not seem any doubt that supernatural tests were used in the trial of crimes,[37] as well as torture,[38] and ordeal by imprisonment with wild animals.[39]

The overall categorizing of crimes by the Inca, into the more severe and the less severe, also gives one some insight into Inca standards. The worst crimes were those considered to be against the Inca, and were called *capaocha*.[40] These included such things as having had relations with a woman of the Inca, or the Sun, or the *acllas*,[41] or having performed witchcraft against the Inca, or having failed to pay tribute. Such crimes were punished by the *ochacamayo,* and by other Inca officials.[42] These crimes were distinguished from others. Rowe has asserted that all breach of law was regarded as disobedience to the emperor, on a par with treason and sacrilege: therefore all crime was punished with severity.[43] The statements in the sources which support this do not seem to be correct, since there was a clear distinction between crimes against the Inca and crimes not against the Inca. An act perpetrated against the Inca, his property, or his authority was a far greater crime than the same act against a citizen. In addition to other penalties, all one's property was confiscated if the crime was against the Inca.[44] The law of homicide gives some indication of this distinction between crimes. Valera mentions that the most extreme form of the death penalty was imposed on one who killed the "king or queen or prince"—the descendants of such a murderer being in disgrace for generations.[45] The law of theft also illustrates this point dramatically.

Cobo tells us that one who stole food from the fields out of necessity was pardoned if the fields did not belong to the Inca, but if they were the Inca's fields, he was put to death.[46] Theft of property of the Inca or the Sun, however small the stolen thing, was penalized by death; [47] but this does not seem to have been the case at all if the object stolen was not of the Inca or Sun.[48] The fact that restitution absolved a finder from accusation as a thief [49] even suggests that perhaps in the ordinary case a thief claiming to be a finder might save himself from punishment. The number of sources in which the theft of food out of need is mentioned suggests that everyone was neither prosperous nor satisfied in the Inca paradise. Food, either stored or in the fields, probably would have been the object most easily stolen and least easily identified or retrieved, even in a small community.

One's own culture seems to be the standard by which the severity of a criminal system is judged. But it is worthwhile to look at the Inca criminal law with a less contemporary and self-centered eye, to forget the whole question of severity, and to examine it to see what it can tell one about Inca culture in general.

No criminal law is a self-contained system. In specifying the types of behavior which are not tolerated, it tells something of general practice and standards and its enforcement shows the governmental machinery at work.

Inca criminal law has striking characteristics which reflect in a single application much that was true of the social and political system as a whole. The emphasis on the sacredness of government, its symbols, its property, its officials, the punitive distinctions made among criminals on the basis of rank and sex; the reservation to the central government of the power to condemn to death; the emphasized use of physical rather than economic punishment; the comparative lack of state concern for the individual as against the overwhelming concern that government remain unchallenged; the same seen in the existence of administrative review rather than appeal; the pervasive belief in supernatural punishment and in supernatural tests of crime; the frequent lack of administrative specialization; the placing of sexual acts on a level of culpability comparable to that of the most serious crimes meriting the death penalty— all these are characteristic of Inca criminal law, yet they have innumerable implications for Inca ideals, standards and behavioral norms. They serve to inform more precisely of the type and level of Inca development.

In comparing Chibcha, Inca, and Aztec lawbreaking, Trimborn sees the possibility of differentiating phases of development of the high culture state, and ascertaining the legal mentality that goes with it. He notes a developing shift from self-help to state enforcement. He also concludes that deterrence gradually replaced revenge as a motive for punishment, and asserts that an older "objective" test gave way to a "subjective" phase in which the state of mind of the lawbreaker was taken into account. He charts a reconstructed evolutionary history of punishment. In Trimborn's view, the death penalty was the original and sole penalty in some primal culture. Step by step in his scheme are added (in order): restriction of freedom, corporal punishment, penalties to honor, and fines and compensation for damage. The Inca rate high on such a scale, the Aztec still higher.

Yet to much of this one must take exception. Underlying it there is an implied concept of the civilized mind as the opposite of the primitive. Has any people ever had a wholly subjective or wholly objective set of criminal law standards? Is there no question of deterrence being involved in retaliatory blood feud as well as revenge? Can one assume that revenge is not a significant element in the state enforcement of criminal penalties? Has it not, for example, been made clear from the studies supporting the abolition of the death penalty, that its deterrent effect is questionable?

It is not the evolutionary element in Trimborn's approach, per se, which raises question, but the way it is used. There is no denying that law has evolved from simpler forms to more complex ones, and that there is a general historical trend which can be discerned from the comparison of peoples of various cutural levels. Hoebel has put it this way in his excellent discussion:

As for law, simple societies need little of it. If the more primitive societies are more lawless than the more civilized, it is not in the sense that they are *ipso facto* more disorderly; quite the contrary. It is because they are more homogeneous; relations are more direct and intimate; interests are shared by all in a solid commonality; and there are fewer things to quarrel about. Because relations are more direct and intimate, the primary, informal mechanisms of social control are more generally effective. Precisely as a society acquires a more complex culture and moves into civilization, opposite conditions come into play. Homogeneity gives way to heterogeneity. Common interests shrink in relation to special interests. Face-to-face relations exist not between all the members of the society but only among a progressively smaller proportion of them.

for supposing that markets were a matter of little or no concern to the central government. This seems quite possible since local markets had absolutely no effect on, or relation to the central government or its tax system.

This prevalence of local barter by housewives in the Inca Empire is in dramatic contrast to the great commercial development of Aztec Mexico, where there were full-time professional merchants. Everything from slaves to food was sold in the Mexican markets, and there were police to keep order and to enforce the standard weights and measures. In Tenochtitlan there were twelve judges to arbitrate the disputes of the market place. All goods brought to the market for sale were taxed, and there were goods whose exchange value was so standardized as to make them able to be used virtually as money. Cacao was one of these standard commodities. It is sometimes said that coca was used the same way in Peru [63] but this is probably post-Spanish, for we are also told that the common people were allowed the use of coca only with permission [64] and that the coca plantations were all owned either by the Inca or by the *caciques*.[65]

Why were there no judges, no standard weights and measures, no taxes, and no police in the markets of Inca Peru? The absence of legal material relating to Inca trade suggests only one probable reason why the Spanish chroniclers should have described Mexican markets in these terms and failed to do so in Peru: that they did not exist in Peru. Comparison of Mexican market practice strongly suggests that the difference between markets in Aztec Mexico and Inca Peru is not to be attributed solely to the confining effects of the Inca government "monopoly of commerce"; but to general differences of economic development.

SUCCESSION AND INHERITANCE

The Spaniards had a peculiar concern with the rules of succession and inheritance. They used them to establish the property claims and the governing rights of the Spanish crown as legal successor to the Inca kings. The delicacy of this concern was tempered by self-interest, which resulted in the Spaniards seeing the Inca rules as they wished to see them. A characteristic answer in the "Informaciones" solicited by Toledo states first that the inheritance of the positions of *curaça, cacique,* or *principal* was subject to the limitation that the successor have the necessary qualifications and ability. This was in fact the rule. But the faithful answerer contradicts himself and distorts the rule to suit, saying that it was the custom to give the *curacaships* and *caciqueships* as the Inca wished without regard to descent or succession. This was plainly not the rule.[66] But it suited Toledo and he argued on this basis [67] that the King of Spain consequently had the right to assign all *cacicazgos* to those who seemed to him most able, and that there being no heirs to the Inca, the Spanish throne could distribute all the property of the Inca.

The Spaniards particularly desired to rationalize away all competitive claims, and to this end saw Inca succession and inheritance as governed by no rules at all. The legacy which this distortion has left to modern scholarship is a general minimization of the hereditary nature of Inca governing classes and has made all the more possible the myth of Inca bureaucracy.

A letter of Toledo's to the King of Spain summarizes the results of his "informaciones." He says that before Topa Inca Yupanqui conquered the Indians, they had only war chiefs and paid no taxes—that they had no real government. Topa Inca Yupanqui is said to have appointed all the *curacas* and *caciques* since none existed before, and to have appointed their successors entirely on the basis of ability. The reasoning which follows is that as the Inca were not legitimate rulers, and the *caciques* were not the natural lords of the land, and, moreover, as there were no legitimate successors of the Inca tyrants, everything belonged to the King of Spain.[68]

What appears to have been the case concerning inheritability of office is that the specific individual to succeed was not fixed, but that it was to be a son or a brother or a nephew seems quite clear. The deep motive of the Spaniards in trying to clear their consciences of any prior claims can account for a good deal of the confusion in the "informaciones" on this point. They often say offices were not inheritable, and then indicate which relatives of the incumbent were eligible to inherit if suited for office. The contradiction undoubtedly arises from several factors: (1) There was regional variation of rules of inheritance.[69] (2) There were rules which did not specify which of a particular group of relatives was to succeed, but allowed the most fit to be chosen. (3) There was a strong Spanish motive to show non-inheritability of which the men answering the "informaciones" must have been aware.

That the inheriting person was not precisely fixed is far from unique to the Inca. The Aztec had a similar system. In England the inheritance of kingship and property inheritance went through a considerable period of flexibility before the more familiar rules of the present day were settled.

There is no way around innumerable indications that the Inca rulers and the valley kings they conquered were members of hereditary aristocracies which the Inca used and perpetuated.[70] The Spaniards chose to see something else. They had good material reasons for doing so and their conclusions need not be heeded too strongly in view of the more plausible contradictory evidence found in the "informaciones" themselves as well as in the principal chroniclers.

The main inheritable tangible property included: [71]

(1) the house and yard;
(2) personal property;
(3) women;
(4) livestock;
(5) lands.

The commoners had a house and yard and personal effects. Polygamy was not permitted them. Private livestock and lands, though they could be obtained as special rewards, or perhaps kept by special grace of the Inca emperor, were probably not usual. The rights to a share of communal land and flocks, though not inheritable in as personal a sense as the other things, ought to be mentioned here because of the kinship basis of the communal landholding unit.

The *curacas* had all of these types of property, and in quantity. There appear to have been some differences in rules of inheritance which depended on the level of rank. Rules governing inheritance from an Inca emperor, for example, differed from the rules governing the *curacas*.

Where the sources indicate that there is any distinction in the rules of inheritance which depends on the nature of the property inherited, it will be mentioned. Unfortunately the information available is rarely as specific as one might desire.

The Inca methods of inheritance and succession may themselves have provided some part of the motive for Inca imperialist expansion. Perhaps the most important inheritable right in the Inca empire was rank. Intangible property itself, it was accompanied by tangible property rights. Tax exemptions connected with rank were inheritable by all sons, not only the successor son.[72] Upper class polygamy and the rules governing inheritance of rank combined to produce a steadily expanding non-taxable class, to be supported by the taxpayers' production and labor. This may have given a strong motive for empire expansion, as it would have put pressure on for a steady increase in tax workers and revenues. Sumptuary laws restricted certain luxuries to this class.

Virtually all the chroniclers describe certain sumptuary laws,[73] litter bearing, the wearing of certain cloth and certain ornaments and jewels, and the privilege of polygamy as belonging to the Inca ruling class and to other persons who were granted these privileges by the Inca.[74] Doubtless, the most important of these were the non-Inca ruling classes. Sumptuary rights went on the whole with rank, and rank was inheritable.

These sumptuary laws can be looked upon as the dramatic symbols of a far more basic kind of class legislation. The inheritance of rank, in many cases accompanied by official positions, property rights in land, and the right to use a certain amount of tax-labor were fundamental. This fact, already discussed, is mentioned here again only to emphasize that sumptuary privileges, though in themselves merely luxurious perquisites of rank, were the superficial signs of the caste system. The upper caste was not solely differentiated by ornaments and numbers of wives, but in everything—from property rights to status before the criminal law.

The succession to government posts, from the Inca down, and the inheritance of land are closely linked.[75] Lands, or at least land rights, appear to have gone with office. Cobo and Falcón say that all administrative posts in the decimal system below the provincial governor and excepting the leaders of 50 and 10 were hereditary, subject to the question of fitness.[76]

A number of the chroniclers assert that there was no fixed rule about who was to succeed, but that the incumbent in office named the man he thought most fitted for the job. Sometimes they assume that the successor would be picked from among the sons of the official, as for example, in the case of the Inca, sometimes from the next lowest rank of official (which may have included sons) [77] as in the case of the *curaca* of a *guaranga*.

First, as to Inca succession itself. The Inca was succeeded by the son of his principal wife whom he designated on the basis of fitness.[78] Acosta [79] says the brother of the Inca succeeds and then his nephew, the Inca's son. Murúa [80] says the brother of the Inca ruled if his son were a minor, and that the brother succeeded if there were no legitimate heir. The Spaniards came on the scene of a civil war about the succession. The dispute was between the sons of Huayna Capac, who had not publicly named his heir before his death.[81]

As for Inca inheritance, it is repeatedly stated that a new

Inca did not inherit the property of the preceding Inca.[82] This certainly at least referred to all personal property, clothing, gold and silver vessels, and to the palace. Each Inca had to build his palace and accumulate his treasure for himself. Castro gives the impression that even land was not inherited, and that fields remained designated as of the first Inca, the second Inca, etc.,[83] and continued to be worked for the benefit of the mummified ancestor and his "household." [84] In spite of Castro, it does not seem possible that this was true of all Inca fields over the empire, though one must admit that a number of the sources just cited could be understood to mean this. Surely it applied at least to certain fields needed to maintain the palace-shrine,[85] and the women and household servants of the dead Inca.

The sons of the Inca who were not sons of his sister, but of his other women were given lands (probably during the Inca's lifetime), and they were clothed and otherwise provided for out of the storehouses.[86] It would seem likely that they did not receive anything additional at the time of the Inca's death.

Below the Inca in the hierarchy were the four *apocuna*, whose offices also tended to be inheritable according to Cobo.[87] The governor's post is omitted from Cobo's discussion of hereditary offices, and seems generally so. If it was entirely an appointive position, it was the only office in the decimal hierarchy to be so.

In Cabello there is evidence that can be interpreted as referring to the inheritability of the governorship. He reports that among the "caciques governadores, y mandones" the eldest son of the Inca-given wife succeeded, failing this heir, the next born brother, and if there were no heirs, the Inca named another person suitable for the post.[88]

Regarding the succession to offices and estates of decimal officials below the rank of *t'oqrikoq* down to that of *pachaca camayos*, Cobo [89] and Falcón [90] tell us that if the eldest son of a *cacique* were able, he was given his father's post. If he were not capable, and the second son showed ability, the second son got the job. If there were no able sons of age, the brother of the dead man succeeded him for his lifetime, and at his death the nephew who earlier had not succeded because of his minority then succeeded. Offices below *pachaca camayo* were appointed and not inherited.

An early *relación* asserts that in the succession to *caciques* posts there was local variation in the rules followed, in some provinces the nephew inherited, in some the sons, in others the brothers.[91] Acosta says the *curacas* had the same rule of succession to office and property as he gives for the Inca. This would be the inheritance by the son, or the brother, and then back to the brother's nephew, the original *curaca's* son.[92] Cieza indicates [93] that there was local variation in inheritance of office—in some places going from father to son, in others from a man to his sister's son.[94] Bandera says that the *caciques* in their lifetime indicated which son was to be the heir and the heir received the best part of the estate, the rest of the sons dividing what remained equally among them at his death.

This account goes on to say that if a man died without leaving heirs, the governor's lieutenant (called *"micho"*) was sent to the house to record in the presence of the local *cacique* the quantity of property by *quipu*. He then reported to the governor who disposed of it as he saw fit.[95]

Castro and Ortega Morejón tell us that among the *curacas* of *pachacas* or *guarangas,* the rule was followed that if the successor was of his *pachaca,* he inherited all the lands, clothing, women, and flocks. This land was like an entailed estate in that it could not be wasted or disposed of, and from it provision was made for all the sons of his predecessor. But if the inheritor was not of his section (*parcialidad*), he inherited the office (*Señorio*) only.[96] He also tells us that the *guaranga* chose the best of his *pachacas* to succeed him. And that the lord of a valley named one of his *guarangas* to succeed him. Thus he goes on to say, they had no rule that it went to the son, nor the uncle, nor the brother, nor the nephew.

Santillán also describes successors in office chosen from the next lower rank irrespective of relationship as applied to the *curacas* of *guarangas* (1,000), and *pachacas* (presumably 500), and then goes on to state that "there is some variation, for others say that these very *curacas* of *pachacas* and *guarangas* are succeeded by the most able brother and this even if there were sons; and then after the death of the brother, the sons of the first brother succeeded." The property which went to the successor of the original *curaca* was used to support his widow and sons as well as the incumbent in office.[97] He also says that the Spaniards completely disregarded the rights of the sons and allowed all property interest to go to the successor of Spanish choice. There appear to have been law suits about this brought by sons against Spanish-appointed officials.

De las Casas says the incumbent in office named the most able successor among his sons, or, if he had none, his brother, or if he had no brother some other able person.[98] He also speaks of inheritance by females,[99] though Cieza [100] for the same place (Huancavelicas) speaks of the inheritance by the son, failing sons the brother, failing brothers the sister's sons. Most probably De las Casas misunderstood this matrilineal alternative to mean inheritance by a woman rather than through a woman.

A confusing account of the La Paz region [101] which generalizes about the empire, says that the position of provincial governor was not hereditary, but that governors were appointed by the Inca from among the principal *curacas* of the province. This is inconsistent with the more usual statement that the provincial governor was of the Inca caste, while the officials under him were of local families. The same account says that succession to *cacicazgos* was largely from brother to brother, or from nephew to uncle (?), and that rarely did the son inherit directly without the interposition of an uncle or cousin.

Garcilaso [102] speaks of variations throughout the empire, mentioning inheritance by the eldest son, alternatively by the most liked son, by the sons in order of seniority, and then back to the son of the eldest son.

Rowe [103] is certainly right when he says that the evidence for descent in the male line is overwhelming in the inheritance of public office. The indifference of the Inca government to local variation is easily understood. Having the power to dispose of any *curaca* who did not do a satisfactory job, it can hardly have mattered what was the local method of succession.

The levirate was practiced; a brother inherited his brother's wives.[104] Bandera [105] also says that the son inherited the wife of his father.[106] As the *curacas* and other ranking officials were permitted more than one wife, while commoners had only one, it is quite understandable that these practices should have prevailed more among officials than among commoners as stated by Lizarraga.

Lands bestowed by grace of the Inca to reward someone for service to the state were granted in tail and passed to the descendants of the first holder, the senior kinsman dividing it at sowing time among the male kindred present per capita.[107] Such lands could not be otherwise divided, exchanged, alienated, or disposed of in any fashion. The inheritance of lands or flocks received as rewards may not have differed very much from the succession to lands connected with office. In the first case land was inherited in common by all male descendants. It was inalienable and indivisible, but distributed for cultivation by the senior kinsman or head of the *ayllu*. In the second case, land was inherited by the successor in office, but Castro, Ortega Morejón, and Santillán say that provision had to be made out of it for all the male descendants of the previous incumbent.[108] According to Castro and Ortega Morejón, lands went with the office when the successor came from the same *parcialidad,* that is, when the office was inherited. Presumably the lands stayed in the kin and local group even if the office did not.

Castro tells us that the commoner having adult sons left his *hazienda* (probably meaning the house and yard, not any agricultural lands) to the most able one and this son took over all the responsibilities of his father. The wife, he asserts, never inherited, but was herself inherited.[109]

What emerges fairly clearly from the somewhat inconsistent and fragmentary assortment of rules concerning inheritance of property and succession to office, is that there was a steadily expanding landed and property-owning class in the Inca empire whose holdings and rights were passed along from one generation to the next. Local variations in rules of inheritance suggest a stability of property rights dating from a pre-Inca conquest period in the more developed regions. Mention of the inheritance of lands with office strongly confirms the thesis that the conventional conception of an Inca bureaucracy is a myth.

IV · THE POLITICAL SYSTEM AND ITS JUDICIAL FUNCTIONS

Inca officialdom, as traditionally pictured, forms a pyramid. The Inca sits at the top of his official hierarchy; below him are the four *apocunas* who ruled the four quarters of the empire, and below them the *t'oqrikoq* who each ruled 40,000 families. Below these are increasing numbers of officials, each governing smaller and smaller subunits, the rulers of 10,000 families (*hunu*), of 1,000 families, of 100 families, and of 10 families (*chunca*).

The Inca emperor is the peak of the pyramid. Standing in a line at the bottom are the headmen of 10 families. In theory, geographical units of the empire corresponded to population units, and the number of officials was fixed according to the number of the taxpayers.

Horacio Urteaga has made the traditional view graphic in his article on Inca judicial organization.[1] Some such pyramid has been described by all the major chroniclers and most recent writers and lecturers on the Inca.[2] Some descriptions include the category of "chiefs of 50 families" and "chiefs of 5,000," which Urteaga omits. But this is a detail. Orderly, mathematical, and easily remembered, such a schematic representation is acceptable both to those who see the Inca Empire as a strongly centralized state, and to those who see it as predominantly under local control. Whatever one's opinions of the Inca, everyone can agree that it does represent the decimal system.

It should be borne in mind, however, that a pyramidal diagram can be made of almost any hierarchical organization, irrespective of what it does or how it works. No illustration of this type can show qualitative characteristics of power and function, neither for the government as a whole, nor as between the various officials. There is, for example, no way to show the strong tendency toward hereditary office-holding. Yet this type of material is the substance of Inca government.

And such a diagram omits several important things it could and should reveal. It fails to indicate any visual distinction between administrators of Inca lineage and those of local origin. The Inca were invaders and conquerors. In each new territory they superimposed Inca government on an already existing one. The degree of governmental development of the conquered peoples varied, but in many instances it appears to have been considerable, as for example in the Chimu kingdom. The Inca altered the apportionment of some of the land, but they did not do away with the local government and replace it. They did not disturb local hereditary interests.[3] They simply added themselves at the top and made full use of the already existing administrative machinery,[4] incorporating the local hereditary aristocracy into the decimal system.

Inca officials probably were drawn principally from the eleven royal *ayllus,* though some may have come from a group of Quechua speaking tribes to whom membership in the Inca class had been granted as a privilege. These "Incas" as they all were called by the chroniclers were the nucleus from which the empire expanded.

The *t'oqrikoq* was the lowest official who had to be an Inca. To represent the government hierarchy as if it were of homogeneous nationality, is to picture it in terms of what may have been the Inca objective rather than in terms of Inca achievement. The Inca emperor doubtless took the sons of local rulers to live at the court at Cuzco with this in mind.

The second major fault of the decimal administrative pyramid is that it leaves out an important group of officials. Both the Inca and his governors had staffs of officials other than the decimal administrators, whom they used as a constant check on, and supplement to, the activities of local officials. Field inspectors, special delegates—traveling and possibly even resident—were used for census, tax, judicial and other matters. Some were assigned only in emergencies, while others were sent out in the ordinary course. Neither the Inca nor the Inca governors had to depend solely on the avenues of administration of the decimal hierarchy.

Writers on the Inca have given little attention to these inspectors and representatives of the Inca government, probably because it is difficult to draw a systematic picture. The sources only contain sporadic references, but these are enough to show their importance, particularly in dealing with cheating or interference with conscription and taxation. The powers and duties of most officials from the Inca down were deeply involved with the tax system.[5] This is true both of those in the decimal hierarchy and those outside it.

The decimal hierarchy itself implicitly reveals the overwhelming preoccupation of the empire government with taxes. The number of governmental officials in the hierarchy was fixed by the number of taxpayers, not by the number of persons in an area.[6] The stated purpose of the great Inca census was to facilitate taxation and the related conscription.[7]

Combining the facts already mentioned with the government's focus on taxes and conscription, one sees the administrative structure in a functioning capacity. The Inca did not destroy the governments of the people they conquered; they sat on top of them and used them. Capitulation always involved a specific agreement to pay tribute. Incorporation of the existing governments into the decimal system facilitated taxation and conscription, and the employment of inspecting and accounting officials outside the decimal system assured the central government that the conquered people were being kept to their tax obligations and not fomenting any rebellions.[8]

In spite of the fact that the sources say the Inca imposed their law wherever they ruled,[9] this must not be naïvely understood to mean that laws affecting all matters were changed on conquest, even though it is stated clearly that laws were universal in the empire.[10] Many local differences of custom seem to have been tolerated.[11] The Inca government does not seem to have tried to stamp them out, much as it did not seek to stamp out local religious cults. Wide Andean cultural continuity rather than political invasion may account for many general characteristics.

Where there are basic cultural differences, the standardization of law is difficult. It is difficult with writing, let alone without. But the Andean area probably was one of essential cultural continuity, and the Inca *quipus* were well suited to recording the kind of numerical information necessary for an extensive tax and conscription program. In these matters, universal method throughout the empire was entirely feasible.

The *quipus* may have been used as mnemonic devices to aid the memory of those to whom the knowledge of traditions and law was entrusted. However, even in our civilization, with writing and professional specialization, legislation and precedent often remain vague and ambiguous. *Quipu*-recorded laws could hardly have been very precise. Much was undoubtedly left to judicial discretion.

What the Inca government primarily insisted on as law was the universal acceptance of its authority, and its officials and its taxes,[12] and as a part of this, the acceptance of the Sun cult, and of the Quechua language. The emphasis was on the acceptance of Inca rule rather than on accepting any particular body of Inca law as such. Clearly many laws were involved in the acceptance of Inca rule, but the emphasis is important.

The obedience to Inca government was not a task left to take care of itself. As we have seen, inspecting, checking and spying by the central government was part of the enforcement system. The other part of the enforcement system consisted of *mitimaes,* placed principally in the capitals of provinces.[13] They were under the control of the Inca ruler of the area, namely the governor. *Mitimaes* were bound to put down any native rebellion that might occur.[14] They also enforced other aspects of the Inca's rule, including the tax requirements.[15]

The *mitimaes* were agricultural families from an old loyal province, resettled in a newly conquered one. Sometimes this involved an exchange of populations. Punishment awaited any *mitima* Indian who did not care for his lot. If he left the place where the Inca had settled him, he was liable to torture for the first offense; for the second attempt he was killed.[16] In the event of a rebellion of the *mitima* Indians themselves, it was hoped that the local populations would remain loyal and could be used by the governor to suppress the insurrection.

It was probably the fear of local rebellion that prompted the resettling of the *mitimaes* in the first place, rather than any planned cultural assimilation of conquered peoples.[17] There was in fact a studied attempt to keep the *mitimaes* from being assimilated into the local population. They were obliged by law to retain their separateness. They continued to dress in the manner of their province of origin.[18] They continued to speak their language of origin.[19] Dances, songs, and music were also kept.[20] In Huamachuco, and presumably elsewhere, the *mitimaes* brought their own *huaca* with them.[21] Everyone, not only the *mitimaes,* was required to wear some distinctive local costume.[22] There was a penalty for altering one's form of dress.[23] Poma says it was 100 blows.[24]

This is an instance of giving legal bite to what probably was a general local custom anyway. The penalty seems considerable until one understands that the evasion of tax obligations would be the most likely motive for trying to alter one's geographical identity.

The *mitimaes* were given land to work and sites on which to build their houses.[25] Cobo states that they were given certain privileges which made them appear more noble, as warriors were.[26] Apparently some of the *mitimaes* were craftsmen and herdsmen rather than agriculturalists.[27] Presumably the Inca governors brought with them some of their own people for skilled crafts. In Huamachuco a great number of the *mitimaes* were of Inca lineage and came from Cuzco.[28] Cobo also reports that among the *mitimaes* there were always many *orejones* (reference to ear deformation as a mark of rank) of Inca blood.[29]

Apparently the *mitimaes* were supported in part by the local population for the first two years of their resettlement—the natives being obliged to build their houses and to give them two years assistance in their fields, and to give provisions from the Inca storehouses for the same period.[30]

The extent of the moving of populations is a crucial, though finally unprovable factor in one's evaluation of Inca government. One can take the view that the Inca virtually put in a central government spoon and stirred up the Andean populations in an effort to mix them into homogeneity, moving huge groups of people from one end of the empire to the other. But this is inconsistent with all the evidence of local stability. It also seems inconsistent with the separateness which the *mitimaes* were supposed to maintain. It is worth bearing in mind the difference between colonization of an area (consider even modern colonialism) and complete assimilation of a population and its culture. Colonists separate themselves from colonials in order not to become assimilated.

The *mitimaes,* who were colonists and potential soldiers in case of rebellion, have been confused with garrisons (which were not colonist) and with colonists, who were in no sense functioning as potential garrisons.[31] Since the Spaniards designated all newcomers and foreigners [32] as *mitimaes,* and since they also called the valley settlers from highland villages, and the colonists *mitimaes,* there is considerable uncertainty as to what the Inca resettlement of populations really amounted to quantitatively. There is no doubt or argument about the fact that it was at least extensive enough to supply the provincial governors with a substantial potential police-military force in the capital cities. As such the colonists deserve inclusion in any schematic picture of Inca government. Like the inspectors and spies, they stand outside the decimal system. But like the inspectors and spies, the colonist garrisons gave force to Inca rule.

It is apparent that in the case of *mitimaes*—and thus potentially in any case—location of residence could be dictated by the central government without regard to the choice of the individual. As for coercion, one may argue that the colonist *mitimaes* were given sufficient inducements to make their lot attractive, but what of the local populations they replaced? The threat of punishment or execution for leaving the place of settlement awaited the dissatisfied. But equally important, the rigid and immobile nature of the agricultural structure was such that a fleeing family could not easily get itself incorporated into an established community.

The resettlement of peoples should be seen, then, as an indication of the way in which Inca imperial power was adapted to the Andean socio-economic structure. The closed cooperative agricultural communities are part of a familiar primitive agricultural pattern, as is the lack of any laboring class for hire. Inca power was built and limited by this structure. It is because of these characteristics that, once resettled by the Inca or his governors, agricultural villages resumed their previous life in a new location.

Lack of economic surplus may be indicated by the fact that except at certain border points where there were true garrisons, the *mitimaes* were resettled villages of agriculturalists and their families, rather than armies of occupation doing a tour of duty. The maintenance of a non-productive army is a burden we know too well. It may not have been skill at the arts of government, or a show of amazing royal power to move whole villages rather than armies. It may have been the only possible way to have a potential garrison in the economic circumstances. It may also be that the exchange of populations had as much to do with land shortage as with the more political motives usually assigned to it.

The Inca state was able to accomplish this shift of peoples because of—and not in spite of—the nature of the sedentary agricultural communities. The power of the state, as usual, shows itself in this case to be dependent on the coincidence of a great number of factors, quite apart from the theoretically absolute legal powers of a divine right monarch.

As head of the government and divine ruler the Inca has been described as having absolute power. "Nothing existed or took place in the realm except by the will of the Inca." [33] There are in the sources many variations on this patent exaggeration.[34] This was the myth, created and perpetuated by the Inca government.

The Inca cannot have ignored what Canute demonstrated— that there are things a king cannot ordain. And it is not only against the forces of the physical world that a king may be impotent. The ideals, the standards, the practices, the culture of the people he rules, on the whole rule him also. And the wider his empire the more power he must delegate to others.

Even when the ruler retains the power to appoint and remove, as the Inca apparently did, he depends on his governors as much as they depend on him. In the Inca empire while most high offices tended to be hereditary, they carried the reservation that appointment and maintenance of office depended on fitness.[35] The Inca succession itself involved some consideration of fitness.[36]

Yet though he could "hire and fire," the Inca's discretion was, in practice, very much tempered by advice.[37] There must be significance also in the number of methods of spying and checking on lower officials, of the use of *mitimaes* garrisons, and of the existence of the civil war into which the Spaniards stumbled. The Inca's power, though divine and legally absolute, seems to have been enjoyed vigilantly and uneasily.

Crimes of officials were handled by the Inca and his court when it concerned an official of the rank of *hunu* or above. Officials below this rank were tried by the governors and inspectors.[38] It is noteworthy that Inca officials alone had judicial power over officials of every rank.

The size of the empire surely affected the administrative structure in a profound way. In spite of a remarkable system of communication,[39] geographical separation and size required a rather considerable delegation of power. One senses a great reluctance to delegate power, however, and the attempt to reserve as much authority as possible to the Inca himself.

A symbolic retention of complete power was kept even when in reality much authority had been effectively delegated. A striking example is that of the use of sumptuary articles. Once a year, the provincial governors came to Cuzco bearing some tribute, and were prepared to report on conditions in their part of the country. In turn the Inca distributed sumptuary articles among his governors. The governors could use certain sumptuary articles (*cumbi* cloth, for example) only when they came from the Inca as gifts, and could not have them made directly for themselves.[40] That they enjoyed their position only by grace of the Inca thus was reiterated annually.

For the most part the great wealth of the provinces in agricultural and herding produce never left the provinces. Though it belonged nominally to the Inca, in practice it probably supported the governors and their households. This was the reality. Yet the sumptuary articles which the *t'oqrikoq* brought with them to Cuzco may be thought of as symbolic of their status. Available only by grace of the Inca, they were a reminder of the retention of control by the Inca.[41]

The attempt to attribute to the Inca far-reaching personal control over matters which concerned every subject is seen in the rule that no man in the realm could marry without solemnization by an official Inca ceremony. It was as if the Inca owned all the women in the empire and gave them away as a matter of grace. In fact, the loveliest women of the empire were chosen for the Inca from the rest, and gathered together in well guarded houses—some to be virgins of the Sun, others to be used for the Inca's pleasure or to be given away by him when he wanted to reward his followers or to show them honor. The Inca could have had no possible direct interest in the marriage of the women who were not "chosen." Yet the marriage ceremony was a symbolic way of asserting that all women could have belonged to the Inca, and that even the lowliest commoner enjoyed his wife only by grace.

These examples show some of the ways in which the myth of Inca omnipotence was continued in spite of the fact that his government bowed to political realities as much as any other. The conflict between having to delegate power out of practical necessity, yet wishing all power to reside in the imperial will is an important aspect of Inca rule. This may have something to do with the rapid extension of the Inca realm. A king can have close personal control if his kingdom is tiny. But by the time the Spaniards saw it, the Inca ruled quite a large empire.

The power to tax and the way the power was exercised show concretely the interaction of Inca absolutism with practical considerations. It also demonstrates the workings of Inca governmental structure. Cobo [42] and Polo [43] tell us that the only measure of the tax was the will of the Inca. Yet insofar as agricultural and herding produce are concerned, the Inca tax was determined by the quantity of land and herds designated as "Inca." Alone the produce of these lands and herds went into Inca storehouses. It was not the amount of agricultural produce which was fixed as tax,[44] but rather the amount of land to be worked [45] or herds to be tended. The size of the Inca lands probably remained fixed from the time of conquest of an area.[46]

The amount of the total agricultural tax, then, was not annually determined in Cuzco, but rather the use that was to be made of a part of it. It was in other matters that the Inca had more discretion, namely in the determination of how many men would be required to do *mita* service. *Mita* service in general seems to have referred to unskilled manual labor, while other work (craft or specialized) was regarded as a substitute for *mita* service. But the Inca did not arrive at his *mita* tax demands capriciously. He had complete census and production figures at his disposal [47] and consulted his council and his governors. [48]

As it was necessary to feed and clothe and supply with tools or weapons any people who were drafted, the financing of a big *mita* draft depended on more than census figures. It depended on what had been accumulated in the Inca storehouses.

The discretion of the Inca and his councilors therefore was applied to two major aspects of the tax system: the size of the empire man power draft, and the use of stored supplies. In the case of man power, the amount of the tax, that is, the number of men called up, over and above those necessary for regular local projects (like normal agricultural work, road repair, post running, and the support of the local government) probably was decided by the Inca and his council. However, the quantity of stored supplies was in certain basic matters fixed, and the choice was as to how and when these supplies should be spent. Cloth, weapons and other man-made tax articles, however, seem to have been made to meet requirements fixed for a particular year. [49]

The situation suggests that the Inca and his councilors in Cuzco would tend to press for empire projects, while the provincial governors might well prefer to yield as little of their stores as possible to non-local enterprises. The Inca consequently had a direct interest in checking closely on the expenditures of the provincial governor. No doubt the Inca and his councilors had the last word in the matter.

A major question is whether, when the *t'oqrikoq* constructed buildings in the provincial capital, he used labor recruited from his province, or labor recruited on a national scale. In short, how often was the labor draft on a national scale resorted to? One suspects that this was the case only for the greater glorification of Cuzco and its environs (such as in the construction of Sachsahuaman) and for armies, but that other projects were accomplished on a provincial level. The original cutting through of the two royal roads also may have been done with a national labor draft, but it is possible that these were built as they were maintained—by the localities through which they passed.

Most important is the fact that there was much local *mita* service, or substitute for *mita* service. From the service of local officials, to the repair of roads, from the craftsmen in the governor's provincial capital to the miners in provincial mines— all were local people serving local public works. The provincial governor spent some of the storehouse contents which were produced by Inca lands [50] and herds. These he must have used, largely to feed and supply with materials all the local craftsmen and *mita* workers. He was obliged to have supplies for armies passing through, yet *mitimaes* [51] had to support themselves after a few years of *mita* help from the local population.

A striking example of an empire-wide *mita* system operated locally was that of the post runners, who were stationed at short intervals along the royal roads. The local villages supplied the men, houses, and supplies for this arduous duty, and the runners were shifted monthly.[52] Even in an imperial plan this kind of local responsibility is characteristic.

All public works may have been technically for the Inca, and taxes of the Inca, but a good deal of discretion must have rested with the provincial governors and their subordinates, not only in the administration of the labor draft, but also in the decision of what was to be done, and they must have profited considerably from what was produced. Since the Inca received annual reports from the provincial governors and his own investigators, doubtless the Inca could veto local projects he disapproved, but plans for these may have been initiated by the governors.

The status of provincial officials is far clearer when considered in relation to *mita*-service than when seen only as a particular rank in an empire hierarchy. Much *mita*-service and some substitutes for *mita*-service were carried out locally under Inca rule. Communal public works, a likely concomitant to communal agriculture were undoubtedly of pre-Incaic origin. To have put this old local labor draft system on an imperial scale is a remarkable achievement and has been much commented upon, but there is no reason to inflate it to include the enormous amount of *mita* service done locally, the pattern of which was basically pre-Inca.[53]

The Inca political achievement is precisely in the extension of local government methods to an empire. In the decimal system itself, one sees the ultimate record of this idea.[54] The number of taxpayers governed is considered the measure of rank rather than any other quality of jurisdiction. There are bigger and bigger numbers up the pyramid. But in fact, size itself results in qualitative differences and the delegation of power, which has been mentioned, is one of the forces of change.

Governing from Cuzco, the capital city, with the Inca, were the four *apocunas,* who composed the council.[55] As in tax matters, one may wonder whether the Inca ever undertook a major decision without at least the advice of the *apocunas.* Each of the four *apocunas* was the top administrator of one of the "four quarters" of the empire. They apparently had power to decide all but the most difficult questions without consulting the Inca, and were important in deciding when to wage war.[56] Some of the Inca's official decisions were made on the basis of divination[57] which suggests a crucial role for the diviners. The elders of the Inca *ayllus* also may have had some advisory role.[58] In Urteaga's pyramidal scheme they achieve an importance just beneath that of the four *apocunas* as a formal tribunal of twelve judges.

Cuzco and the Inca were the focal point of the empire government. Contact with empire affairs was maintained through the reports of the provincial governors, which in any hurry could be conveyed through the very efficient post-running system, but which regularly were made every year in person; and the reports of inspectors and special delegates sent directly from Cuzco. Inspections by officers sent out by the Inca to the provinces are recorded as taking place every three years,[59] every two years,[60] and annually.[61] Regular inspections are also mentioned without time interval.[62] Special occasional delegates also seem to have been sent out from the capital.[63] This makes it clear that Cuzco had a double system for acquiring the information necessary for government.

The decimal hierarchy, then, basically composed of local non-Inca administrators, was constantly checked on by officials whose principal loyalty was to the central government. Interestingly enough, some or perhaps all of these inspectors were fed and clothed by the *curacas* of the valleys they were inspecting.[64] It is not surprising that the Inca or his governors could dispatch investigators or special delegates when events required. But that there should have been regular arrangements for checking local conditions, outside the decimal hierarchy is worthy of much more notice than has been accorded it.

With respect to the punishment of crimes affecting the government, there appears to have been a close connection between the reports made by annual inspectors and the sending out of judges by the central government with power to punish.[65] These judges were sent out when the inspectors disclosed that there had been violations of law. The judges punished crimes and fixed penalties as they saw fit, and were not bound by any rules as to the applicability of particular penalties.[66] The *ochacamayo*, as these judges apparently were called, used divination and torture when more rational methods of obtaining information were unsatisfactory. They apparently received presents from the local *curaca* when they came on their much-feared business. Santillán speaks of special investigator judges called *taripasac*.[67]

The Inca government apparently appropriated jurisdiction of all matters affecting it, and acted directly through judicial agents of the central government rather than through the decimal hierarchy in these cases. This is another significant underlining of the difference between conqueror and conquered, and another instance of by-passing the decimal administration.

Indirectly this brings out a fundamental characteristic of Inca administrative structure: Higher officials had power to invade the offices of lower officials. This was, of course, most true of the Inca himself. Whenever the Inca was present, he alone was the judge before whom all wrongs were pleaded. When he was not present, justice was administered by his governors and *caciques*.[68] One has the strong impression that the Inca could take any matter out of the governor's hands if he chose. In fact, in any difficult or complex matter, the governor was obliged by law to consult the Inca.[69]

In the same manner the provincial governor could intervene in the official life of his province. Officials beneath the rank of *t'oqrikoq* had to get permission from the governor to impose the death penalty,[70] and they kept their superiors informed of events in their jurisdiction. It was an uneasy delegation of power, all the way down the line.

Two major characteristics of Inca government on the Inca level are thus seen. First, that the ordinary administrative structure was incompletely relied on, and provision made to check it constantly, and on occasion to have others act in its place. And second, that higher offices might invade lower ones and perform duties ordinarily assumed to be in the jurisdiction of the lower official. The emphasis on supervision and rank seems to be characteristic.[71]

The basic outlines of the Inca pattern were repeated on the

level of the *t'oqrikoq*. That is, what the Inca was in relation to the empire, the governor was in relation to his province. As such the *t'oqrikoq* headed the regular administrative hierarchy, and also acted through a second branch, a set of special officials directly responsible to the governor and not to anyone within the administrative ranks. The governor had a staff of accountants (*quipucamayos*) who kept records for him.[72] There is mention in the sources of visiting inspectors or judges who made temporary trips from the provincial capitals.[73] Bandera says that in the province of Guamanga the *tucuyrico* had a subordinate called a *micho* stationed in every major town (this may refer to a subordinate of the *tokoyrikoq*), whose job it was to handle some civil matters.[74] These concerned the boundaries of the lands and farms and the irrigation ditches and waters, and other minor controversies between the pueblos. The *micho* also handled cases of intestacy.[75] This does not seem to refer to the officials of the decimal system. Not only did the governor have official subordinates outside the decimal system, but he also had a police-military force. Against rebellion or refusal to pay taxes the Inca governors could rely on the support of the *mitimaes*. Surely this potential military and police force should be regarded as part of the Inca government, though it is never depicted in the schematic presentations of the same.

In view of the foregoing it is not quite so remarkable that few of the governing offices in the decimal hierarchy were occupied by the Inca themselves, while many were in the hands of the very local rulers whom the Inca conquered, or their descendants or kinsmen.[76] Cooperation with the Inca ruler was probably the necessary condition for remaining in office, and the extensive system of checking and by-passing assured that any unreliability would soon be discovered. Whether this actually worked dependably from the Inca's point of view is another question. That there was great concern with rebellion and tax cheating is shown by the precautions taken. These fears probably had a foundation in fact.

One assembles the descriptions of the Inca provincial governor with the reservation that, as Rowe has pointed out,[77] there probably has been confusion between the Quechua names for the *t'oqrikoq*, the provincial governor, and the *tokoyrikoq*, a government inspector sent to the provinces to check local conditions. The *micho* referred to above may, for example, have been an underling of the inspector (*tokoyrikoq*), rather than of the governor.[78]

Annually at the feast of Raymi, the *t'oqrikoq* went to the court, reported the state of affairs in his district and presented to the Inca the tribute which had been required from his area.[79] He supervised all the rulers of smaller units of population, and had charge of the raising of armies, the census taking, the tax collection, and the Inca and Sun lands in his province.[80] The provincial governor also had powers to administer justice and to punish crimes.[81] He had judicial powers in all criminal cases relating to the Inca, witchcraft, or speaking against the Inca, Indians fleeing the place where they were supposed to live, and any neglect of the *tambos* or neglect of duty by the *chasquis*. He could sentence by himself if he did not consider it an important enough case to refer to the Inca.[82] According to Cobo [83] he could impose the death penalty as he saw fit, except in a case involving a noble, in which instance he was obliged to consult the Inca, which he also did in all difficult and important matters.[84]

When criminal trials were conducted by the governor all persons concerned or having any knowledge of the delict were assembled. They sat in a circle with the accused in the center. Each one stated his accusation. The defendant then had an opportunity to deny and explain. If the result was uncertain the governor sent to the man's *curaca* to discover whether he had a good reputation. If the answer was negative, he was tortured until he confessed and then was punished appropriately.[85]

Officers beneath the rank of the *t'oqrikoq* could not impose the death penalty without permission from above. Cobo tells us that a *cacique* who killed an Indian subject of his without permission, even if it was for cause, was severely punished.[86]

The power to impose the death penalty independently seems to have been nominally reserved by the Inca to himself, but was probably in fact given to officers appointed by him, that is, the *t'oqrikoq* and the *ochacamayo*. However, subordinate officials apparently could apply the penalty with permission.

The *hunus* and lower officials had cognizance of lesser offenses. They had charge of the allocation of land, and where the land was irrigated, of water. They supervised the mining of gold and silver and the marriage of their subjects in the official annual ceremony.[87]

It is significant that, at least toward the bottom of the hierarchy—if not above—the *cacique* was personally responsible for the performance of tax duties by those in his charge. If there were any omission in the service of the *tambos,* the local *cacique* in charge of the *tambo* was punished for it; [88] and he passed the punishment along to those under him.

Lesser officials accused any offender in their charge, kept the census, and informed their superiors of these matters and of local needs. The higher officials supervised the lesser, particularly guarding against their exceeding their authority.[89] This was in keeping with the general supervision of the district and its affairs.

The unspecialized nature of Inca offices is notable. All functions of government were in some measure invested in each decimal official. There was no separate judiciary except possibly for the special judges sent out by the central government. In the decimal hierarchy, judge, tax collector, and governor were one, and so up and down the line.

One senses that the duties of the governing officers—of whatever rank—were much more emphasized and more clearly defined than their powers. The job of government was to maintain itself, to produce taxes, armies, and to keep the peace, with some national-religious proselytizing thrown in. The powers associated with office were to conduct these affairs in the customary way (about which custom we know miserably little) and with great care not to usurp the power of any higher official. The hierarchy seems to have been very sensitive to disrespect. There was great fear of usurpation of power from below—not surprising for an invader government which has been superimposed on a pre-existing government accustomed to independence. There was great fear of rebellion, and the many shades of incipient rebellion from disrespect to treason.

The modern Anglo-American constitutional concern for the limitation of the power of government and the protection of the rights of the individual are seen here in reverse. The concern in the Inca state was for the protection of government. The great fear was of challenges of its authority. The fear was not that the government would exceed its power, but that it would be weakened by the usurpation of its power by subordinates and subjects.

THE JUDICIAL FUNCTION

Judicial powers appear almost always to have been ancillary to other government functions in the Inca system; hence it is almost impossible to speak of a judicial system. In the decimal hierarchy each governing official had general powers over the territory he governed.[90] The Inca could judge whatever case he wished.[91]

One *Relación* tells of a court of 12 judges from the *ayllus* of Cuzco, 6 from the Hanan moiety, and 6 from the Hurin.[92] The court is said to have had 2 assistants who kept records of the laws on *quipus* and whose learning was handed down from generation to generation. It is curious that if this court did exist it has not been made more of in the major chroniclers.

In the decimal system, the higher the official, the more important to the state were the matters he could decide. Minor local questions and presumably all contentions between individuals were resolved finally at the lowest levels of the hierarchy. There were no appeals.[93] But officials were obliged to report their judicial activities to superior officials as a part of keeping the government informed about what was taking place in the communities.

The provincial governor had judicial powers in all criminal cases relating to the Inca. One may infer that crimes and private contentions in which the Inca government had no such direct interest were tried by the various levels of *curacas*. One would also guess in this case that local customary laws applied.

Although officials below the rank of governor could not impose the death penalty without permission from above, this does not necessarily mean that the Inca conquerors sought to replace the customary rules by which such decisions were arrived at, nor that they themselves fixed the instances in which they were applied. Supervision by the governor is in no way inconsistent with the continued application of local laws to local matters.[94]

In trying to reconstruct the sort of justice which was dispensed at the *curaca* level, particularly in the communities, one should bear in mind that at the lowest ranks, the local *curacas* probably were the senior kinsmen of the kin group, and that there was a face to face relationship within the community.

The *curaca* had charge of allocating the annually divided shares of communal land and dealt with whatever conflicts arose in connection with the individual shares. In conflicts about other property the sources justify the assumption that there was often recourse to the local *curaca* in his judicial capacity. For example, theft was variously punished, depending on the circumstances, by penalties including reprimand, public beating, and death. In all of these instances punishment was an official act; it was not the job of the wronged party to avenge himself.[95] On the other hand, where flocks damaged a field, the owner of the field had the right to take from the herd the equivalent in value of the damage done.[96] Whether disagreement in this case ultimately would result in bringing the matter to the *curaca* is not stated. There is no mention of blood feud. Homicide appears to be entirely a matter for official intervention.[97]

Outside the decimal system were special judges sent out by the Cuzco government to deal with crimes involving a refusal to accept fully the obligations to and authority of the Inca state and the state religion. These ranged from refusal to pay tribute, to witchcraft against the Inca. There were the *ochacamayoc,* judges who were dispatched to punish crimes discovered by the regular investigating officials when the crimes touched on Inca power. The crimes called *capaocha* [98] included having relations with one of the chosen women or women of the Inca or Sun, having performed witchcraft against the Inca, or having failed to pay tribute.[99]

There was the *runaquipo* or *lunaquipo* who was sent out by the Inca state to supervise bringing the census *quipos* up to date. He was empowered to choose men to be *yanaconas* and women for the Inca and Sun. For the crime of concealing anyone from the *lunaquipo,* he could punish with blows of a stone.[100] Santillán speaks of the *taripasac* [101] who also appear to have been concerned with crimes against the Inca, or relating to women for the Inca or the Sun. Some ecclesiastical ranks may also have had judicial powers to investigate and punish crimes in connection with the religious establishment.[102]

One gets the impression from this material that those in charge of checking on and enforcing the various aspects of the tribute system had powers to punish that were incidental to their other functions. This seems to have been true of officials within and without the decimal system.

There would appear to be an overlapping of criminal jurisdiction between the provincial governor and the various officials sent directly from the central government to enforce the

Incaic tribute demands. This does not seem inconsistent with the other functions of both governor and central government envoys which also overlapped. The actual overlapping seems quite probable and not due solely to the semantic confusion between the Quechua names for inspector and governor.

Controversies over the boundaries of large administrative subdivisions appear to have been settled by the sending of a special royal delegate [103] or by the Inca emperor himself. Within the provinces this was presumably one of the functions of the governor since he is said to have had charge of the allocation of lands among the Inca, the Sun, the *curacas* and the Indians.[104] The governor also decided on what disposition was to be made of property when there was no heir.[105]

The number of officials having judicial functions outside the decimal hierarchy was probably greater than those specifically mentioned in the chronicles. A number of Quechua words for various kinds of judges are mentioned in the 17th century dictionary of González Holguín.[106] However, the dictionary is dated 1608. Thus the Quechua language it describes had had numerous years of Quechua experience with Spanish courts to have expanded the juridical vocabulary. Even if many of the terms were pre-Spanish the meanings might have altered, and the definitions given in terms of Spanish offices also might not have been exactly equivalent.

There did exist a customary trial procedure, certainly from the administrative level of provincial governor up the ladder.[107] Yet there were no lawyers and it appears that there were no fees or taxes paid to the Inca in law cases.[108] This suggests a limited development of formal courts.

In a criminal trial if the matter was not clearly settled by testimony, the judge could apply to the *curaca* of the accused for information as to his character.[109] When matters remained in doubt, divination, torture and ordeals were used.[110] There is disagreement about whether or not there was an oath.[111]

In a record so fragmentary as that of the Inca, one hesitates to reach conclusions from the absence of material. However, it may be significant that one hears nothing of regular sessions of courts at particular calendrical intervals on any level. This suggests that matters were tried as they arose. The punitive powers of traveling officials (the various inspectors) indicates the same.

The whole emphasis of function of Inca judges seems to be the attempt by a conquering state to enforce its demands and its administrative arrangements on a population not altogether delighted with the Inca Eden. One reads in the sources that all officials had jurisdiction over all types of legal matters, varying merely in gravity and importance. Yet of the specific examples of justice at the inspectors and the Inca governor's level, virtually all concern the Inca state. There is almost no information on the solution of trouble cases which would expose the law stuff that must have existed at the village level, and which would disclose the extent of regional variation. The information is on the Inca government as conqueror.

THE INCA STATE

The Inca empire is a classic example of the conquest state. But it was by no means the first emergence of the state in the Andean area. In fact it is most probable that the Inca invaders learned much from the advanced peoples they conquered. Rowe [112] has suggested that some techniques of administration, including ruling through a local hereditary aristocracy were adopted from the Chimu empire, conquered in the 15th century by the Inca.

In conquering peoples whose groups varied in size and political development, the Inca apparently had a consciously devised plan of incorporating them into a larger political unit. They tried to impose a uniform administrative and taxation system as well as the Sun cult and the Quechua language. As Professor Lowie has said concerning overemphasis on the growth of the state through conquest: [113]

We must accordingly recognize . . . the importance of ideological factors over and above those of a rationalistic or specifically economic order. It is not enough that one society should defeat another, just as it does not suffice for two societies to share a language or to allow each other's members to join in ceremonial activities. Such conditions may be ancillary, but they are not adequate. What is required is some centralizing authority powerful enough to counteract primitive separatism . . . a . . . frequent method has certainly been the defeat of rival populations, *if followed by their incorporation in a common polity.* Upon this crucial point of organizing ability after conquest the possibility of permanent extension hinges.

The Inca have been justly praised as possessors *par excellence* of the type of administrative ability Professor Lowie mentions. The Inca obviously tried to make their conquests stick. Not only did they subdue a variety of peoples, but at the base of much of the empire were the fundamentally separatist landholding kin groups, which, supplemented by limited local trade, were virtually economically independent. Some of the job had been done for the Inca. Where they conquered people already grouped in some political unit, as they were in much of the empire, the Inca did not hesitate to employ the administrative machinery they found already functioning. The chroniclers tell us again and again that the local rulers were left in office. Where sufficiently large political groupings were not already functioning, the Inca created them. The Inca undoubtedly made some administrative rearrangements and took precautions so that in maintaining previous political units, they did not perpetuate forces that might be used for rebellions.

The organization of the empire into theoretically equivalent administrative sub-units has created an unwarranted impression of homogeneity. Much of the linguistic and cultural diversity survived the Inca conquest. This was no Ashanti kingdom [114] where a number of relatively homogeneous kin units, alike in language and culture as well as in administrative organization, were ultimately joined, from clans into tribes, and finally into what Hoebel has called the "primitive confederated monarchy." [115] The population of the Andean area was of varied linguistic and cultural tradition and has been estimated at from four to eight million persons. The Ashanti population was about 200,000.[116]

The confederated tribal organizations, whether on a simpler scale than the Inca such as the Pueblo or Iroquois, or like the Ashanti and Aztec, appear to have had a much more representative type of government. Tribal councils or councils of nobles representing the various tribes, or villages, clans or lineages, had an important role in government in these cultures. Perhaps the Inca were such a confederated tribal organization a century before the Spanish Conquest, before they began their expansion over the whole central Andean region. The *ayllu* organization around Cuzco, and perhaps the tribunal of 12 judges, 6 from each *ayllu*, were vestiges of such a period. But at the time of the Conquest there were no councils of *curacas*, no council of provincial governors. There was no formal representative body except that perhaps the *apocunas*, each governing one quarter of the empire could be considered such. Annually at the feast of Raymi the governors were said to have come to Cuzco to report to the emperor and present tribute, but there is no mention of their meeting as a body to consider the affairs of state. Though tax assessments of the Inca were announced to an assembled group of the nobility and were then discussed and apportioned,[117] the material does not suggest that the nobility might act as a body to refuse the assessment or to initiate projects. One gets no impression of a legislative assembly in any modern sense.

There are a very few instances in which a royal council is mentioned, and most of these refer to the four *apocunas*,[118] though one or two refer to a larger body of *orejones* (Inca by descent or privilege originating in the Cuzco region). These sporadic mentions do not amount to anything comparable to the regular and dominant role of tribal councils among many other peoples. It does not seem possible that such a body existed and simply escaped notice.

Not only has the theoretical equivalence of all the administrative subdivisions of the Inca empire given an impression of homogeneity; the information on Inca culture has done so also. Rowe has put it plainly: [119]

With minor exceptions, the whole of the literature now available which deals with this part of the Andean area refers to Inca culture in the region around Cuzco, so that it is only for the Inca that a complete cultural description is possible.

Thus, both the type of government plan the Inca created, and the fact that the chroniclers' information on the Inca culture is principally confined to the Cuzco region give the impression that every village in the empire was like every other village, and that all were made to conform to the master plan. What on the surface appears to have been a uniform tripartite system of land tenure, on closer inspection shows itself to have included many interests not mentioned in the plan and to have varied from place to place. The taxation system, based, to be sure, on a census and the equivalence of sub-units, was more than an equal division among the sub-units of lump tax demands made from Cuzco. Each region contributed what it specialized in geographically or professionally. The size of tax lands varied from place to place. The uniformity of plan covered a prickly and irregular landscape of fact.

This is not to say that the use of an administrative plan by the Inca government was not important. It was the abstract expression of an intention to unify the empire. Nor should it be understood that the plan of government did not effect some measure of local reorganization wherever the Inca conquered. It was, the theory by which, to borrow Lowie's phrase, the centralizing authority counteracted primitive separatism, and also coped with cultural diversity.

It is not to debunk the Inca reputation to say that the plan was not the reality, nor does it really detract from the Inca achievement. For a primitive people to have had such a plan in the first place is a considerable political achievement, and to have had the practical realism to adapt it to local conditions is evidence of no mean administrative ability. But to accept the plan as if it were an infallible homogenizing machinery is to attribute something to the Inca that did not exist.

V · INCA LAW, THEORY AND PRACTICE

This book has set out to describe the law and government of Inca Peru, the immediate purpose being to contribute toward a more specific description of Inca culture. In its pertinence to the structure of the state, the information has more general application. A clear purpose for which political power was used by the Inca was to free the ruling caste from restrictions on its sexual, social and economic life, restrictions which it enforced to the extent of the death penalty upon the commoner. Yet the acknowledged objectives of government were peace, plenty, and justice to be given in return for obedience and taxes. As a source of specific information on how these multiple purposes were served and rationalized, the law is far from being a dull bit of formal esoterica. The concrete legal material is suitable ballast for speculative balloons.

It is generally acknowledged that the law is basic cultural material. Yet in defining law as a segment of culture for study, it is difficult not to slice off too thin a slice. A widely accepted current definition uses as its criterion the application of physical force.[1] The definition starts with the norm, but the test inevitably emphasizes the violations rather than the rule.

The negative aspects of this definition usually have been energetically compensated for by adding in one form or another that the law is incomprehensible outside of its cultural context. E. A. Hoebel, for example, quite rightly insists that it is necessary to study the "ideals presupposed by the whole social complex"[2] to properly comprehend the law of a people. These he calls "jural postulates." In his *Law of Primitive Man* he presents jural postulates of several cultures in the form of brief lists, ranging in the included items from such general attitudes as "sexual activity should be held to a minimum," [3] to a quite specific practice such as Trobriand matrilineality.[4]

However one may applaud the cultural emphasis of the postulation theory of law, there is much that is discouraging about trying to apply this method. By what standard are relevant ideals to be separated from the rest of the cultural material? For law, the coercively enforced norm, there is the practical criterion of force. For ideals what is the gauge? If one overcomes this difficulty there is another problem to be met. The listing of condensed jural postulates in itself creates an inefficient body of material that is not comprehensible without further explanation. Jural postulates are hard to catch and still harder to keep alive in captivity. More detailed descriptions of the culture are necessary in any case, hence the more diffuse methods of this book.

Finding social ideals or basic values has been a contemporary preoccupation. From Benedict's "patterns" to Northrop's "key concepts" to Kardiner's "primary and secondary institutions and basic personality type," there is the theme (and it runs through the work of innumerable others) of extracting from a culture its basic values. Boil it down long enough and you will ultimately come out with culture in a bouillon cube, a condensation, an essence, to which one only has to add watery details to reconstitute the original.

There is nothing wrong with condensation if it is done with sufficient care. However, the search for basic cultural values has all too often been undertaken as an eager hunt for what is assumed to be a single necessarily coherent and consistent pattern. This has the consequence of giving insufficient attention to variety and to conflicting values. Law and politics deal with the harnessing of diverse and explosive human materials. The norm and its violation are found together. The leader and the follower exist only together. Conflict is a primary element in law and the stuff of politics, whether it be conflict of ideals, of interests, of authority, or of rules. Diversity, conflict, and instability are as much a part of the social fibre as are harmony and consistency. Nowhere is inconsistency more blatantly and more cheerfully and more universally tolerated than in political matters.

The Inca appear to have been no exception to this rule. At least some of the less successful effort that has gone into trying to categorize the Inca system and make it into a political bouillon cube could have been saved if Inca practice had been separated from Inca political theory. Because we know the political theory sketchily and only through numerous pairs of astigmatic Spanish eyes, its exact nature remains debatable. Yet even this confused material can be sorted out to the extent that the decimal administrative system, the tripartite land division, and other overall schemes emerge as partially applied pieces of political theory. One should simultaneously recognize that the chronicles show clear continuities of local power and property interest inconsistent with these overall schemes, but which fit well in the context of the pre-Inca Andean past.

At this late date, it is difficult to judge to what extent the imposition of the census, decimal and tax systems, the Quechua language, the Sun cult, the Emperor, and the *mitimaes* were intended to weld the empire into a unit, to homogenize it, to reduce diversities, or how much this was merely the elaborated implementing of a tax system which had some of these consequences. In short, were these unifying results planned, or did they come incidental to another end? Both may be partly true. The practice of leaving the powerful in power seems to have stood even though the decimal administrative system did not acknowledge it. The administrative system certainly had centralizing consequences, whether or not this was a principal conscious goal. That a political plan is a rationalization and is incompletely realized does not mean that it is without effect. It is also a truism that the results contemplated by the plan may not be the actual result.

When Luís Valcárcel and Louis Baudin and other distinguished admirers of the Inca emphasize a welfare state element of Inca rule, what they applaud may not be a Spanish invention. This may have been the Inca's view of themselves, however far from economic realities.

Why should the Inca state not have claimed for itself all the virtues of the folk communities it encompassed—as if it had chosen to continue them in existence, or had even created them? The Inca government plan may have been largely a theoretical incorporation of existing institutions into a single scheme. The scheme could easily gloss over many inconvenient realities.

The Inca apparently were skilled in selecting and diffusing what Harold Lasswell has called "justifying symbols in politics." [5] But there is no reason to take protestations of paternalistic motive at face value any more than claims of divine origin. Nor is there any justification for being distracted from the actual power and property elite by the nominal pyramidal system of administration and schematic tripartite division of property which the Inca created. Both the power situation and the political rationalizations that went with it deserve to be fully considered, not as aspects of a static system, but as elements in a continuously changing alignment. The legal material is invaluable in reconstructing this aspect of Inca history, in ascertaining who had power, what it was used for, how it was perpetuated, and which were the likely elements of instability.

Why should those who unembarrassedly claim that the Inca planned their state, and even tried to create one according to some humane ideal, boggle at the acknowledgement that they also had the civilized (and perhaps universal) characteristics of inconsistency and self praise. As Milovan Djilas has said in one of the most recent expositions of the disparity between political theory and practice: [6]

> Every private capitalist or feudal lord was conscious of the fact that he belonged to a special discernible social category. He usually believed that this category was destined to make the human race happy, and that without this category chaos and general ruin would ensue.

The plan itself is an important Inca achievement, regardless of the question of its altruistic or centralizing nature. One can quite easily separate two aspects of the reputed special development of Inca government, the extent to which the plan was realized, whatever it was, and the quality of planning itself. Robert Redfield has said, "The intentional making over of society is a conception of civilized man, perhaps only of modern man." [7] The Inca government plan suggests that the idea of the making over of society is not exclusively the creation of modern man.

An important dimension is added to the study of Inca law and government if it is considered in terms of some of Redfield's concepts. He has traced the fate of the folk society, the small isolated, homogeneous and self-sufficient community. He describes the alterations it undergoes when civilization mushrooms up with its cities and its specialists and its clashes of tradition. In this connection the paradox in the Inca system is obvious. On the one hand, the rural folk society was taken into account. Its inherent conservatism was utilized and the plan sought to keep it isolated and continue it in its customary pattern. On the other hand the folk community was forcefully linked both to a provincial capital and to Cuzco through the imposition of taxes, the Sun cult, the Quechua language and the court and high government. Centralizing and decentralized elements were worked into the same scheme.

The legal material, while it cannot make up for the fragmentary nature of the evidence, does show in a practical sense how pre-Inca local rights and duties were fitted into the Inca political and administrative structure. It thereby shows the Inca administrative talent lay not in the peculiar ability to totally reorganize every foot of land and every group of people to conform to a master plan, but the ability to use what they found, yet alter enough to weld an empire. The study of the practical administration of the Inca legal system and its procedural methods leaves no doubt but that some common assumptions must be modified.

Evidence has been shown here that the bureaucracy was no real bureaucracy; that there is good reason to believe that the administrators held land and were not supported out of Inca tax-stores, their land and government posts being generally hereditary.

The conception of the decimal system of administration as a single pyramidal hierarchy has been demonstrated to be an ideal concept incompletely realized. The pyramid diagrammatically heals the significant breach between conqueror and conquered, and tactfully ignores all the checking and spying and colonizing with potential soldiers (*mitimaes*) that the victors used against the vanquished. The power of the provincial governor to call up the *mitimaes* to suppress rebellion or to enforce the payment of taxes reminds one forcefully of a difference in police power between Inca and non-Inca officials. The office of Inca governor was one of an occupying conqueror. The checking officials and the *mitimaes* give intimations of the less homogeneous aspects of the hierarchy and certainly deserve regular schematic inclusion as a significant part of government.

Except possibly for imperial judicial envoys sent to handle certain state crimes, and the possible existence of a court in Cuzco, there was no separate judiciary and all judicial functions were handled by officials who conducted other affairs of government. This is seen in context when one considers that there were special officials for checking and accounting and dealing with the various aspects of the tribute system. There was no form of appeal, though there was review. The acts of inferior government officers were reported to superiors. One may infer that this was largely to prevent underlings from exceeding their jurisdiction rather than to insure the enforcement of any specific body of law. Judicial development thus appears to have been fairly rudimentary. This is particularly significant since the Inca are often characterized as having reached some zenith in government skills.

The taxation system impresses one with the extent to which the empire was a tribute empire rather than an economically interdependent whole. With its exactions of agricultural production, craft production, man power and women, taxation can be looked upon as one of the central activities of the Inca government. The preoccupation with taxation rather than social planning or paternalism may well have been the foundation of many social achievements. The census can be seen in these terms as can the legal strictures on mobility, both as to class and geography, which were attempts to maintain the sedentary nature of local communities and freeze the class structure.

The elaborate taxation system is coupled with what appears to be the remarkable absence of any government-connected commercial law. This is generally attributed to Inca monopoly. Yet the limited and local nature of trade may have been a result more of the locally-centered community and economic structure, than of any restrictive policies of the Inca government. There was relatively little mercantile development—nothing comparable to Aztec Mexico. Confirmation of the primitive level of trade is found in other aspects of Inca law. Not only were there no "judges of the market" as there were in Aztec Mexico, but it is also significant that standard measures, while applied to the taxation system, have not been found mentioned in connection with the market. Barter between the womenfolk of neighboring villages seems to have been the usual form of trade, even as it is today.

Another indicator of limited commercial development comes from the criminal law where there are but few instances of economic penalties. In Aztec Mexico the punishments for crimes often involved temporary or life slavery, or certain standard payments. One does not find anything comparable among the Inca. Physical penalties were general. Surely the tax burden, the Inca sumptuary laws, and the restrictions on the accumulation of property by non-Inca officials did not encourage the development of trade. Yet can one appropriately speak of restrictive government monopoly where there does not appear to have been any appreciable mercantile development? Such mention would fit too well with the general tendency to attribute Inca social and economic life completely to Inca government planning.

Detailed inspection of the legal rights and duties connected with land and land produce shows the inadequacy of the traditional view that land was held only by the Inca, the Sun, and the communities. The use of specific parts of Sun land for the support of purely local *huacas* is a striking example. The evidence cited that Inca lineages held lands quite separate from the Inca "tax-lands," and that *curacas* held lands, also upsets the neat tripartite division. The celebrated bureaucracy itself is shown by the land law to have been more like a landed ruling class than a salaried civil service.

With respect to the tax system, the integration of conquered territories into an empire does not seem to have been exaggerated nor does the incorporation of local government into an administrative hierarchy. However, inspection of Inca law obliges one to note the limited judicial development, the absence of commercial law and market taxes, the absence of common economic penalties, and the existence of a complex of land rights other than the simple government-planned Inca, Sun, and community division. One is also struck by the pervasiveness of class differences in all aspects of the legal system, be it the type of landholding, taxation and taxability, or status before the criminal law. These all bind the Inca empire to its historical past and modify the master-plan conception of Inca politics and law. Though occasionally the Inca used commoners of ability as government officials, it was within the basic tradition of local stability and inherited power and position. The qualification of competence was ordinarily considered after the candidacy of lineage.

T. S. Eliot has sung the praises of social class stratification as an essential condition to high civilization.[8] For those who find his argument congenial, and think it desirable to preserve through family the segment of culture perpetuated by an upper class, there is some food for thought in the relation of the governing Inca aristocracy to the criminal law. How significant that penalties for all crimes were lighter for the nobility, that what was criminal for the commoner was often not so for the noble, that nobles could expect to be judged by their peers, and that the Inca enjoyed the greatest privilege of all, being virtually incapable of crime, since from incest to homicide, from the taking of property to the transfer of property, the Inca emperor was not bound by the rules which bound others. It may not be that power corrupts, and absolute power corrupts absolutely. It may simply be that power is desirable because it gives license.

The urgently pressing human wish to be free of the usual social disciplines is apparent in the privileges of the Inca emperor and nobility. Restraints on behavior were loosened for one segment of Inca society, while another was left bound. There are countless parallels in other places and times. The idea that the strictest of morals are essentially for the commoner, for those without power, is certainly not unknown today. Yet the economic and moral privileges of the Inca nobility, however exploitative, need not have deterred them in their conception of themselves as the essential civilizers of the Andean area.

This, even though there were high civilizations and developed governments before them. From the evidence of the chroniclers, they considered themselves great altruistic states-

bringers. They may well have had the most ideals, whatever their practice. Multiple thought and action are hardly a modern g that the Inca should in their turn have by a handful of the most fortune-hunting of Spaniards in the name of true religion, true morality, and true civilization.

• NOTES

INTRODUCTION

1. "Inca" is used to describe variously the Inca emperors, the Inca caste, the Inca culture, the Inca empire, and an archeological period. In this book I have endeavored to indicate which I am talking about with each use. Where it is not specifically indicated, the context will make the meaning clear.

2. *Handbook of South American Indians,* edited by J. H. Steward, II, 8.

3. Means, *Ancient Civilizations of the Andes,* p. 350.

4. Bonthoux, *Le Régime économique des Incas.*

5. Marof, *Justicia del Inca.*

6. Trimborn, *Quellen zur Kulturgeschichte,* p. 235.

7. Valcárcel, *Historia de la cultura antigua del Perú.*

8. Wittfogel, *Oriental Despotism,* p. 249.

9. Murra, "Economic Organization of the Inca State," (unpublished MS, University of Chicago).

10. Rowe, "Inca Culture," in *Handbook of South American Indians,* II, 273.

11. Murdock, *Our Primitive Contemporaries,* p. 431.

12. Means, "Biblioteca Andina," in *Transactions of the Connecticut Academy of Arts and Sciences,* XXIX, 271–525.

13. Baudin, *L'Empire socialiste des Inka.*

14. Rowe, "Inca Culture," in *Handbook of South American Indians,* II, 192–201, and 330.

15. Trimborn, *Quellen zur Kulturgeschichte,* p. 228, quotes Garcilaso as saying the Chincha Valley was conquered by Pachacuti. The "Relación" itself speaks of Topa Inca Yupanqui as the first Inca. Topa Inca's reign was c. 1471–c. 1493 though he commanded the army from 1463. Topa Inca's dates are taken from Rowe, "Inca Culture," in *Handbook of South American Indians,* II, 203.

16. See Levillier, *Don Francisco de Toledo,* 3 vols., particularly Vol. II.

17. Means, "Biblioteca Andina," in *Transactions of the Connecticut Academy of Arts and Sciences,* XXIX, 521.

18. The answers to many of the questionnaires have been gathered together by Marcos Jiménez de la Espada in *Relaciones geográficas*. Some appear in the second volume of Roberto Levillier's, *Don Francisco de Toledo*. Some are found in the *Colección de libros y documentos referentes á la historia del Perú*.

19. Means, "Biblioteca Andina," in *Transactions of the Connecticut Academy of Arts and Sciences*, XXIX, 496.

20. The reader is referred to the bibliographical works and comments mentioned previously of Means, Baudin, and Rowe and to Rubén Vargas Ugarte. The dissection and evaluation of the sources is a considerable study in itself. Because late sources borrow freely from earlier ones the citation of two documents is often virtually the citation of a single source. This is frequently the case with Cobo and Polo, with Garcilaso and Valera and with innumerable *relaciones*. Anyone undertaking to use the sources is committed to a complex bibliographical problem, involving difficult questions of relative credibility.

21. Rowe, "Inca Culture," in *Handbook of South American Indians*, II, 183–330.

22. Bram, *An Analysis of Inca Militarism*, p. 37.

23. Steward, "South American Cultures," in *Handbook of South American Indians*, V, 732.

24. See for example Bram, *An Analysis of Inca Militarism*, p. 43.

25. Radin, "A Restatement of Hohfeld," *Harvard Law Review*, 51:1141–1164 (1938); K. N. Llewellyn, "Hohfeld," *Encyclopedia of the Social Sciences* (New York, 1932), VII, 400.

26. *Curacas* were governing officials beneath the rank of provincial governor. The provincial governor was of the Inca caste, while the *curacas* were of local ruling families.

27. *Relaciones geográficas*, II, San Miguel de Piura, 240–41.

28. See Rowe, "Kingdom of Chimor," in *Acta Americana*, VI, 26–59.

I. THE LAND, THE FORMS OF TENURE

1. Baudin, *L'Empire socialiste des Inka*, p. 113.

2. Latcham, "El dominio de la tierra," in *Revista chilena*, LII (1927), 201–57. The record of the law suit he cites is in Vol. 206 of the *Documentos de la Real Audiencia: Archivo Histórico Nacional de Santiago de Chile*.

3. *Relaciones geográficas,* II, San Miguel de Piura, 240–41.

4. The alienation of land acquired when it was unclaimed virgin soil may have been an exception. *Relaciones geográficas,* Quito, III, 97; but the account in which this is mentioned can be understood to allude to post-Columbian conditions.

5. Rowe, "Inca Culture," in *Handbook of South American Indians,* II, 272.

6. Cobo, *Historia,* III, xii, xxviii, 246.

7. Santillán, "Relación," in Jiménez ed., *Tres relaciones,* pp. 47–48. Castro and Ortega Morejón, "Relación," in Trimborn ed., *Quellen zur Kulturgeschichte,* p. 244.

8. *Relaciones geográficas,* II, San Miguel de Piura, 240–41.

9. *Relaciones geográficas,* II, San Miguel de Piura, 240–41.

10. Though the chroniclers sound as if new plots were assigned each year, the statements are not sufficiently unambiguous to rule out the possibility that certain families regularly cultivated certain plots, that is, the annual redistribution was nominal rather than actual.

11. Cobo, *Historia,* III, xii, xxvii, 249–50; Polo, "Relación," in *Colección de documentos inéditos,* XVII, 32 ff.; Garcilaso, *Royal Commentaries of the Yncas,* II, 6; "El gobierno del Inga," in *Colección de libros y documentos,* III, Series 2, 77–86.

12. "El gobierno del Inga," in *Colección de libros y documentos,* III, Series 2, 78; "Relación del origen é gobierno," in *Colección de libros y documentos,* III, Series 2, 61–63.

13. Rowe, "Inca Culture," in *Handbook of South American Indians,* II, 255.

14. Polo, "Relación," in *Colección de documentos inéditos,* XVII, 32.

15. Rowe, "Inca Culture," in *Handbook of South American Indians,* II, 266.

16. Polo, "Relación," in *Colección de documentos inéditos,* XVII, 37–39; Cobo, *Historia,* III, xii, xxviii, 250. Much of the material in this subsection is based on these page references.

17. Cobo, *Historia,* III, xii, xxvii, 246.

18. See notes 37, 38, 39 below.

19. Cobo, *Historia,* III, xii, xxvii, 246; Polo, "Relación," in *Colección de documentos inéditos,* XVII, 17.

20. Rowe, "Inca Culture," in *Handbook of South American Indians,* II, 265.

21. To the same effect Polo, "Relación," in *Colección de docu-*

mentos inéditos, XVII, 18; Acosta, *Natural and Moral History*, VI, xv, 418–19; Castro and Ortega Morejón, "Relación," in Trimborn ed., *Quellen zur Kulturgeschichte*, p. 244.

22. The *huacas* or *guacas* were holy objects, places, or spirits. They often varied from village to village, though some had wider significance.

23. Acosta, *Natural and Moral History*, VI, xv, 418–19.

24. Valera, *Las costumbres antiguas del Perú*, pp. 97, 100; Cobo, *Historia*, III, xii, xxii, 221.

25. Polo, "Report," in Markham ed., *Rites and Laws of the Yncas*, pp. 167–68.

26. Polo, "Relación," in *Colección de documentos inéditos*, XVII, 83–86.

27. Valera, *Las costumbres antiguas del Perú*, p. 106.

28. Polo, "Relación," in *Colección de documentos inéditos*, XVII, 102; *Relaciones geográficas*, I, Guamanga, 102; De las Casas, *De las antiguas gentes del Perú*, pp. 48, 159; *Relaciones geográficas*, III, Loxa, 218; "El gobierno del Inga," in *Colección de libros y documentos*, III, Series 2, 78; Santillán, "Relación," p. 45.

29. Garcilaso, *The Royal Commentaries of the Yncas*, I, 305–6; II, 6.

30. Castro and Ortega Morejón, "Relación," in Trimborn ed., *Quellen zur Kulturgeschichte*, p. 245.

31. Cobo, *Historia*, III, xii, xxv, 234.

32. Cobo, *Historia*, III, xii, xxx, 256; Cieza, *Travels*, 313. See also Acosta (*Natural and Moral History*, V, xv, 332), who does not specify which lands supported these houses.

33. Cieza, *Crónica del Perú*, II, xxviii, 110–11; Cabello, *Miscelánea Antártica*, xv, 311.

34. Cobo, *Historia*, III, xii, xxiii, 247; Polo, "Relación," in *Colección de documentos inéditos*, XVII, 18–19.

35. See Cabello, *Miscelánea Antártica*, xv, 311.

36. Bram, *An Analysis of Inca Militarism*, p. 44.

37. Cobo, *Historia*, III, xii, xxv, 235, 244–46; *Relaciones geográficas* I, Guamanga, 99 and Atunrucana, 188; III, Loxa, 217; De las Casas, *De la antiguas gentes del Perú*, p. 113; Castro and Ortega Morejón, "Relación," in Trimborn ed., *Quellen zur Kulturgeschichte*, p. 243; Santillán, "Relación," in Jiménez ed., *Tres relaciones*, pp. 20, 27, 43–44.

38. Cobo, *Historia*, III, xii, xxvii, 244; Falcón, "Relación," in *Colección de libros y documentos,* XI, Series 1, 152.

39. Cobo, *Historia*, III, xII, xxvii, 246; "Relación del origen é gobierno," in *Colección de libros y documentos*, p. 72; Castro and Ortega Morejón, "Relación," in Trimborn ed., *Quellen zur Kulturgeschichte*, p. 245; *Relaciones geográficas*, I, Atunrucana, 188; Garcilaso, *The Royal Commentaries of the Yncas*, II, 6, 10, 305–6; De las Casas, *De las antiguas gentes del Perú*, p. 113; Santillán, "Relación," in Jiménez ed., *Tres relaciones*, pp. 19–20, 43–44; Falcón, "Relación," in *Colección de libros y documentos*, XI, Series 1, 151; Cabello, *Miscelánea Antártica*, p. 348.

40. *Relaciones geográficas*, I, Atunrucana, 188; Rowe, "Inca Culture," in *Handbook of South American Indians*, II, 261.

41. Valera, *Los costumbres antiguas del Perú*, p. 101.

42. Rowe, "Inca Culture," *Handbook of South American Indians*, II, 261. Rowe seems to assume that the nobility held land only as a reward for special services.

43. Santillán, "Relación," in Jiménez ed., *Tres relaciones*, p. 19.

44. See for example Cobo, *Historia*, III, xII, xxvii, 244–48; De las Casas, *De las antiguas gentes del Perú*, pp. 113, 156–57.

45. Cobo, *Historia*, III, xII, xxviii, 248.

46. Cobo, *Historia*, III, xII, xxv, 235.

47. Garcilaso, *The Royal Commentaries of the Yncas*, II, 1.

48. Castro and Ortega Morejón, "Relación," in Trimborn ed., *Quellen zur Kulturgeschichte*, p. 244.

49. Santillán, "Relación," in Jiménez ed., *Tres relaciones*, pp. 47–48.

50. *Relaciones geográficas*, II, San Miguel de Piura, 240.

51. Rowe, "Kingdom of Chimor," in *Acta Americana*, VI, 27. The kingdom was conquered by the Inca in the second half of the 15th century. "At its greatest extent, the Kingdom of Chimor included all these valleys . . . from Tumbez to Carabayllo," p. 34.

52. Rowe, "Kingdom of Chimor," in *Acta Americana*, VI, 54–56.

53. Polo, "Relación," in *Colección de documentos inéditos*, XVII, 22.

54. Santillán, "Relación," in Jiménez ed., *Tres relaciones*, p. 20.

55. *Relaciones geográficas*, I, 97 and 102; Means, *Ancient Civilizations of the Andes*, p. 310, cites Acosta, IV, xxii; Cobo, v, xxix; Garcilaso, vIII, xv.

56. Cobo, *Historia*, III, xII, xxxvi, 291; Valera, *Las costumbres antiguas del Perú*, p. 105.

57. Castro and Ortega Morejón, "Relación," in Trimborn ed., *Quellen zur Kulturgeschichte*, p. 243.

58. A *hanega* is a variant spelling of *fanega*, by modern standards approximately 1.59 acres.

59. Castro and Ortega Morejón, "Relación," in Trimborn ed., *Quellen zur Kulturgeschichte*, p. 245.

60. To this effect Cobo, *Historia*, III, xii, xxv, 234.

61. Castro and Ortega Morejón, "Relación," in Trimborn ed., *Quellen zur Kulturgeschichte*, p. 245.

62. Rowe's phonetic spelling of the Quechua words for inspector (*tokoy-rikoq*) and governor (*t'oqrikoq*) are used throughout this book to emphasize their difference. For other designations which do not present the same confusion the chroniclers' hispanicized spellings have been used.

63. *Relaciones geográficas*, I, Guamanga, 99.

64. Cieza, *Crónica del Perú*, II, xx, 74.

65. See for example *Relaciones geográficas*, I, Guamanga, 99; Levillier ed., *Gobernantes del Perú*, IX, 272; Murúa, *Historia del origen*, iii, v, 171–73.

66. Cobo, *Historia*, III, xii, xxx, 255.

67. See pp. 61, 62, 68–72 in this book.

68. Murúa, *Historia del orígen*, iii, v, 171–73.

69. Cobo, *Historia*, III, xii, xxvii, 243.

70. Cobo, *Historia*, III, xii, xxvii, 245.

71. Cobo, *Historia*, III, xii, xxvii, 246.

72. See pp. 54–58 in this book.

73. Cieza, *Crónica del Perú*, II, xx, 74.

74. Cieza, *Crónica del Perú*, II, x, 32–34.

75. Cieza, *Crónica del Perú*, II, xi, 37–38.

76. Cieza, *Crónica del Perú*, II, xviii, 69.

77. Cieza, *Crónica del Perú*, II, xi, 37–38; Sancho, "Relación," in *Los cronistas de la conquista*, p. 179.

78. Cabello, *Miscelánea Antártica*, xx, 360; See also Cieza, *Crónica del Perú*, II, lxi, 233.

79. Cobo, *Historia*, III, xii, xxviii, 250.

80. Cobo, *Historia*, III, xii, xxviii, 250; Polo, "Relación," in *Colección de documentos inéditos*, XVII, 37.

81. Rowe, "Inca Culture," in *Handbook of South American Indians*, II, 261; Valera, *Los costumbres antiguas del Perú*, p. 101.

82. See pp. 27–31 in this book.

83. Cieza, *Travels*, p. 241; Cobo, *Historia*, III, xii, xxx, 254–55, 257.

84. Cieza, *Travels,* p. 313; De las Casas, *De las antiguas gentes del Perú,* p. 158; Levillier ed., *Gobernantes del Perú,* p. 291; Cobo, *Historia,* III, xii, xxv, 234.

85. "Declaración de los quipocamayos a Vaca de Castro," in *Colección de libros y documentos,* III, Series 2, 18.

86. Cobo, *Historia,* III, xii, xxxi, 260–65.

87. Cieza, *Crónica del Perú,* II, xix, 72; "El gobierno del Inga," in *Colección de libros y documentos,* III, Series 2, 78.

88. Castro and Ortega Morejón, "Relación," in Trimborn ed., *Quellen zur Kulturgeschichte,* p. 245.

89. Steward, "South American Cultures," in *Handbook of South American Indians,* V, 732–35.

90. Rowe, "Inca Culture," in *Handbook of South American Indians,* II, 265.

91. Cobo, *Historia,* III, xii, xxviii, 247; Polo, "Relación," in *Colección de documentos inéditos,* XVII, 18–19; Acosta, *Natural and Moral History,* VI, xv, 419.

92. Acosta, *Natural and Moral History,* VI, xv, 419; Cobo, *Historia,* III, xii, xxx, 254.

93. *Relaciones geográficas,* II, San Miguel de Piura, 240.

94. Castro and Ortega Morejón, "Relación," in Trimborn ed., *Quellen zur Kulturgeschichte,* p. 244.

95. See Rowe, "Inca Culture," in *Handbook of South American Indians,* II, 324.

96. Castro and Ortega Morejón, "Relación," in Trimborn ed., *Quellen zur Kulturgeschichte,* p. 244. A *fanega de sembradura* is the amount of land necessary to sow a *fanega* of seed, approximately 1.60 bushels. *Fanega de tierra* is by modern standards a measure of approximately 1.59 acres. We can assume that Castro's *hanega* is a variant spelling of *fanega.*

97. Rowe, "Inca Culture," in *Handbook of South American Indians* II, 266 and 324; Garcilaso, *Royal Commentaries of the Yncas,* II, 9–10. For a discussion of the size of the *tupu,* see Baudin, *L'Empire socialiste des Inka,* p. 90.

98. Steward, "South American Cultures," in *Handbook of South American Indians,* V, 732 .

99. Castro and Ortega Morejón, "Relación," in Trimborn ed., *Quellen zur Kulturgeschichte,* p. 245.

100. Castro and Ortega Morejón, "Relacion," in Trimborn ed., *Quellen zur Kulturgeschichte,* p. 244.

101. Garcilaso, *Royal Commentaries of the Yncas*, II, 1.

102. Cobo, *Historia*, III, xii, xxix, 251; Polo, "Relación," in *Colección de documentos inéditos*, XVII, 54.

103. Cobo, *Historia*, III, xii, xxix, 251.

104. Polo, "Relación," in *Colección de documentos inéditos*, XVII, 102–3; Cobo, *Historia*, III, xii, xxix, 253; xxv, 279; Santillán, "Relación," in Jiménez ed., *Tres relaciones*, p. 23.

105. Polo, "Relación," in *Colección de documentos inéditos*, XVII, 55–56; Cobo, *Historia*, III, xii, xxix, 253.

106. Poma, *Primer nueva corónica*, p. 186.

107. Poma, *Primer nueva corónica*, p. 186.

108. Cobo, *Historia*, III, xii, xxvi, 241.

109. Cieza, *Travels*, p. 288.

110. Cobo, *Historia*, III, xii, xxv, 236.

111. Castro and Ortega Morejón, "Relación," in Trimborn ed., *Quellen zur Kulturgeschichte*, p. 245.

112. Cobo, *Historia*, III, xii, xxvi, 240.

113. Valera, *Las costumbres antiguas del Perú*, p. 106.

114. "El gobierno del Inga," in *Colección de libros y documentos*, III, Series 2, 78.

115. Cobo, *Historia*, III, xii, xxxvi, 291.

116. See also Cobo, *Historia*, III, xii, xxv, 236.

117. Valera, *Las costumbres antiguas del Perú*, p. 105.

118. De las Casas, *De las antiguas gentes del Perú*, p. 199.

119. Garcilaso, *Royal Commentaries of the Yncas*, II, 42.

120. Rowe, "Inca Culture," in *Handbook of South American Indians*, II, 246; Root citing Garcilaso in *Handbook of South American Indians*, V, 205.

121. Root, in *Handbook of South American Indians*, V, 205.

122. Cobo, *Historia*, III, xii, xxxi, 262.

123. Xerez, "Verdadera relación," in *Crónicas de la conquista del Perú*, pp. 50–52; Xerez, in H. H. Urteaga ed., *Los cronistas de la conquista*, p. 39.

124. Baudin, *L'Empire socialiste des Inka*, p. 173, cites Estete in Xerez, "Verdadera relación," pp. 334 and 338, and Pizarro, *Carta* (Trad. angl.), p. 121.

125. Polo, "Relación," in *Colección de documentos inéditos*, XVII, 39.

126. Cobo, *Historia*, III, xii, xxviii, 248, also speaks of an abundance of land.

127. Polo, "Relación," in *Colección de documentos inéditos*, XVII, 41.

128. *Relaciones geográficas*, III, Loxa, 218, and III, Quito, 98. The records of these cases, if any exist, would be a productive source on Inca land organization.

129. *Relaciones geográficas*, III, Quito, 98.

130. *Relaciones geográficas*, II, Piura, 241, and III, Quito, 97.

131. *Relaciones geográficas*, I, Atunrucana, 184, and III, Otovalo, 111.

132. See Chap. IV of this book. Garcilaso, *Royal Commentaries of the Yncas*, I, 149–50; Cobo, *Historia*, III, xii, xxv, 232–37.

133. De las Casas, *De las antiguas gentes del Perú*, p. 173; Cobo, *Historia*, III, xii, xxviii, 246.

134. Cobo, *Historia*, III, xii, xxviii, 247; also concerning penalties for removing landmarks, Levillier ed., *Gobernantes del Perú*, IX, 285.

135. Valera, *Las costumbres antiguas del Perú*, p. 94.

136. In the Quito region, we are told that to acquire rights to virgin land a man had only to go to the *cacique* and say "those lands be so and so's." Or as an alternative he could take possession and cultivate it, and once this was done and it was ascertained that no one had previously laid claim to the land, his rights were protected. The fact that the account says such possession carried with it the right to sell or alienate, suggests that the entire procedure may be post-Spanish. *Relaciones geográficas*, III, Quito, 98.

137. Castro and Ortega Morejón, "Relación," in Trimborn ed., *Quellen zur Kulturgeschichte*, p. 243; *Relaciones geográficas*, III, Cuenca, 189.

138. Cobo, *Historia*, III, xii, xxviii, 248, 250.

139. Acosta, *Natural and Moral History*, VI, xv, 419; Polo, "Relación," in *Colección de documentos inéditos*, XVII, 21; Valera, *Las costumbres antiguas del Perú*, pp. 56, 115, 116; Santillán, "Relación," in Jiménez ed., *Tres relaciones*, p. 47. Bandera, in *Relaciones geográficas*, I, Guamanga, 102; "Horden que el Ynga tubo en la governación," (unpublished MS, British Museum, Fol. 413).

140. Baudin, *L'Empire socialiste des Inka*, pp. 103–4.

141. Cunow, *Die Soziale Verfassung des Inkareichs*, p. 96; Trimborn, "Der Kollektivismus der Inkas," in *Anthropos*, XVIII–XIX, 978–1001; XX, 579–606.

II. THE TAX SYSTEM

1. Rowe, "Inca Culture," in *Handbook of South American Indians*, II, 265; Cobo, *Historia*, III, xii, xxvii, 245; Valera, *Las costumbres antiguas del Perú*, p. 108; Poma, *Primer nueva corónica*, p. 338.

2. Cobo, *Historia*, III, xii, xxvii, 243.

3. Murra, "Economic Organization of the Inca State," (unpublished MS, University of Chicago).

4. Cobo, *Historia*, III, xii, xxvii, 243–46.

5. Cobo, *Historia*, III, xii, xxvii, 246; Santillán, "Relación," in Jiménez ed., *Tres relaciones*, pp. 43–44; Falcón, "Relación," in *Colección de libros y documentos*, XI, Series 1, 151; Garcilaso, *Royal Commentaries of the Yncas*, II, 5; De las Casas, *De las antiguas gentes del Perú*, p. 113.

6. Animals could be owned by individuals in tail, like land. Polo, "Relación," in *Colección de documentos inéditos* XVII, 102; Cobo, *Historia*, III, xii, xxix, 251–53.

7. Cobo, *Historia*, III, xii, xxv, 246; Santillán, "Relación," in Jiménez ed., *Tres Relaciones*, pp. 43–44.

8. *Relaciones geográficas*, I, Atunrucana, 188.

9. Valera, *Las costumbres antiguas del Perú*, p. 111; Cobo, *Historia*, III, xii, xxxi, 265; Estete, "Noticia del Perú," *Los cronistas de la conquista*, p. 246.

10. Cobo, *Historia*, III, xii, xxvii, 245.

11. See pp. 112, 119 in this book.

12. Cobo, *Historia*, III, xii, xxviii, 249.

13. Cieza, *Crónica del Perú*, II, xviii, 68–69.

14. De las Casas, *De las antiguas gentes del Perú*, pp. 113, 157.

15. Polo, "Relación," in *Colección de documentos inéditos*, XVII, 61, 62.

16. Cieza, *Crónica del Perú*, II, xviii, 68.

17. Polo, "Relación," in *Colección de documentos inéditos*, XVII, 27.

18. Polo, "Relación," in *Colección de documentos inéditos*, XVII, 107.

19. Castro and Ortega Morejón, "Relación," in Trimborn ed., *Quellen zur Kulturgeschichte*, p. 244.

20. Polo, "Relación," in *Colección de documentos inéditos*, XVII, 58–61; Valera, *Las costumbres antiguas del Perú*, pp. 39, 43; Murúa,

Historia del orígen, III, xxxvi, xlii, xliii; Cieza, *Crónica del Perú,* II, xxvii, 106–7; Garcilaso, *Royal Commentaries of the Yncas,* I, 303–4; "Relación del origen é gobierno," in *Colección de libros y documentos,* p. 63; Acosta, *Natural and Moral History,* V, xv, 332; Jerez, "Verdadera relación," in *Crónicas de la conquista del Perú,* p. 51; Molina, in *Las crónicas de los Molinas,* p. 21; Borregán, *Crónica,* p. 80.

21. Cobo, *Historia,* III, xii, xxxv, 279.

22. *Relaciones geográficas,* San Miguel de Piura, II, 240.

23. Cobo, *Historia,* III, xii, xxvii, 243–46; see also Falcón, "Relación," in *Colección de libros y documentos,* XI, Series 1, 153.

24. Cobo, *Historia,* III, xii, xxvii, 245. For a list of skilled occupations see Poma, *Primer nueva corónica,* p. 191.

25. Rowe, "Inca Culture," in *Handbook of South American Indians,* II, 265–69.

26. Rowe, "Inca Culture," in *Handbook of South American Indians,* II, 268.

27. Cobo, *Historia,* III, xii, xxvii, 245; see also Acosta, *Natural and Moral History,* VI, xvi, 421–22; Garcilaso, *Royal Commentaries of the Yncas,* II, 46; Valera, *Las costumbres antiguas del Perú,* p. 109.

28. "Relación del origen é gobierno," in *Colección de libros y documentos,* p. 65; Cobo, *Historia,* III, xii, xxx, 257.

29. Valera, *Las costumbres antiguas del Perú,* p. 109.

30. See also Cobo, *Historia,* III, xii, xxvii, 244; xxx, 257; Castro and Ortega Morejón, "Relación," in Trimborn ed., *Quellen zur Kulturgeschichte,* p. 244.

31. Cieza, *Crónica del Perú,* II, xix, 73.

32. Cobo, *Historia,* III, xii, xxxvi, 291. Cieza mentions silver mines in the province of Huárez worked for the Inca as tax (Cieza, *Travels,* p. 293), and later (p. 385), speaks of silver mined in the province of Charcas by the Indians "for their lords."

33. Valera, *Las costumbres antiguas del Perú,* p. 105; Cobo, *Historia,* III, 273; *Relaciones geográficas,* I, Guamanga, 102.

34. Cobo, *Historia,* III, xii, xxvii, 245.

35. Cobo, *Historia,* III, xii, xxvii, 244; xxx, 257; Castro and Ortega Morejón, "Relación," in Trimborn ed., *Quellen zur Kulturgeschichte,* p. 244.

36. Probably a tapestry cloth with feathers woven into it. See Rowe, "Inca Culture," in *Handbook of South American Indians,* II, 242.

37. Cobo, *Historia*, III, xii, xxv, 234.

38. Cobo, *Historia*, III, xii, xxx, 257.

39. See for example, Cieza's description of Xauxa and the many craftsmen working for the temples and palaces there. (*Travels*, 297–98).

40. Cieza, *Crónica del Perú*, II, xiv, 49–51.

41. Cieza, *Travels*, 329.

42. Castro and Ortega Morejón, "Relación," in Trimborn ed., *Quellen zur Kulturgeschichte*, p. 245; Cieza, *Crónica del Perú*, II, xviii, p. 69; "Relación del origen é gobierno," in *Colección de libros y documentos*, p. 63.

43. De las Casas, *De las antiguas gentes del Perú*, p. 113; Cobo, *Historia*, III, 245, 255, 256; Polo, "Relación," in *Colección de documentos inéditos*, XVII, p. 20; Valera, *Las costumbres antiguas del Perú*, p. 109.

44. Described by Bernard Mishkin, "The Contemporary Quechua," in *Handbook of South American Indians*, II, 419 and referred to by Rowe in the same volume, p. 255. Among the modern Quechua, this is a method of exchanging labor for labor, around which cooperative work parties are organized.

45. Valera, *Las costumbres antiguas del Perú*, pp. 108–12; Garcilaso, *Royal Commentaries of the Yncas*, II, 20; Cobo, *Historia*, III, xii, xxvii, 243–46.

46. Santillán, "Relación," in Jiménez ed., *Tres relaciones*, p. 71, says that if one did not have a wife, one was not obliged to give tribute in cloth.

47. Castro and Ortega Morejón, "Relación," in Trimborn ed., *Quellen zur Kulturgeschichte*, p. 245.

48. Cieza, *Crónica del Perú*, II, xviii, 69; Cabello, *Miscelánea Antártica*, xix, 347, xx, 360.

49. Castro and Ortega Morejón, "Relación," in Trimborn ed., *Quellen zur Kulturgeschichte*, p. 245.

50. Santillán, "Relación," in Jiménez ed., *Tres relaciones*, p. 22.

51. "Relación del origen é gobierno," in *Colección de libros y documentos*, p. 63.

52. Cieza, *Crónica del Perú*, II, xv, 54.

53. Cobo, *Historia*, III, xii, xxv, 234.

54. De las Casas, *De las antiguas gentes del Perú*, pp. 113, 157.

55. Cobo, *Historia*, III, xii, xxx, 255.

56. Cieza, *Travels*, pp. 286, 290, 330; De las Casas, *De las antiguas*

gentes del Perú, pp. 47–49, 157, 159, 160; *Relaciones geográficas,* I, Guamanga, 102; Molina (Chile), *Las crónicas de los Molinas,* p. 22.

57. "Relación del origen é gobierno," in *Colección de libros y documentos,* pp. 61–63; "El gobierno del Inga," in *Colección de libros y documentos,* p. 78.

58. Cieza, *Crónica del Perú,* II, xix, 71–73.

59. Cieza, *Crónica del Perú,* II, xv, 54; Cobo, *Historia,* III, xii, xxxi, 260–65; Estete, "Noticia del Perú," *Los cronistas de la conquista,* p. 246, deals with community obligation to build and repair roads in the vicinity; Valera, *Las costumbres antiguas del Perú,* p. 111, on similar obligation to repair irrigation works.

60. See pp. 24–26 in this book.

61. Cobo, *Historia,* III, xii, xxx, 258. Cf. also sources cited by Baudin, *L'Empire socialiste des Inka,* p. 177.

62. Some writers insert a "rulers of 5,000" category which would add another 400 *mita* workers to the total. I have not included this bonus 400 partly because the "ruler of 5,000" is in many instances omitted by authoritative sources, and partly in order not to prejudice the results too extravagantly in my favor.

63. Cobo, *Historia,* III, xii, xxvii, 245.

64. A closer knowledge of Inca agricultural economics than this writer possesses might indicate just what percentage of the population had to be in food production to support itself and the rest. From this alone could one judge the accuracy of these figures. There must have been a substantial surplus. Its size is the question.

65. Estimates of population for the Andean area at the time of the Conquest range from 12–15 million down to 3 million. (Steward, "South American Cultures," in *Handbook of South American Indians,* V, 656.)

66. As a provincial governor theoretically ruled over 40,000 taxpayers, I am assuming the population size of a province to be 5 times this figure, choosing 5 arbitrarily to be the size of each taxpayer's family.

67. Steward, "South American Cultures," in *Handbook of South American Indians,* V, 732.

68. Cobo, *Historia,* III, xii, xxx, 254; Polo, "Relación," in *Colección de documentos inéditos,* XVII, 28.

69. Cieza, *Travels,* p. 134.

70. See pp. 35–37 in this book.

71. Cieza, *Crónica del Perú*, II, xix, 71; Cobo, *Historia*, III, xii, xxiv, 227–29; xxx, 258; Valera, *Las costumbres antiguas del Perú*, pp. 110–11.

72. Cobo, *Historia*, III, xii, xxiii, 269–74.

73. Cobo, *Historia*, III, xii, xxx, 258.

74. Cobo, *Historia*, III, xii, xxiv, 274; Polo, "Relación," in *Colección de documentos inéditos*, XVII, 68–69.

75. Polo, "Relación," in *Colección de documentos inéditos*, XVII, 68.

76. See also Cobo, *Historia*, III, xii, xxvii–xxix, 243–58.

77. Polo, "Relación," in *Colección de documentos inéditos*, XVII, 58–61.

78. Cobo, *Historia*, III, xii, xxiii, 272.

79. Cobo, *Historia*, III, xii, xxvii, 245; xxi, 255, 256.

80. Cieza, *Crónica del Perú*, II, xviii, 69.

81. Betanzos, "Suma y narración," in *Biblioteca Hispano-Ultramarina*, V, x, 60–62; xiii, 81; xvi, 108. Murúa, "Historia de los Incas" in *Colección de libros y documentos*, IV, Series 2, iii, xliii, 225.

82. Acosta, *Natural and Moral History* VI, xiv, 416, 418; Cobo, *Historia*, III, xii, xxxiii, xxxiv, 269–274; Santillán, "Relación" in Jiménez ed., *Tres relaciones*, p. 46; Polo, "Relación," in *Colección de documentos inéditos*, XVII, 67.

83. Cieza, *Crónica del Perú*, II, xviii.

84. Cieza, *Crónica del Perú*, II, xviii, 68–69.

85. See for example Polo, "Report," in *Rites and Laws of the Yncas*, pp. 167–71.

86. Cieza, *Crónica del Perú*, II, xviii.

87. McCown, *Pre-Incaic Huamachuco*.

88. Cobo, *Historia*, III, xii, xxvi, 241; Levillier, ed., *Gobernantes del Perú*, IX, 274.

89. Cieza, *Crónica del Perú*, II, xviii, 70.

90. For a discussion of the persistence of the institution of the *cacique* throughout Peruvian history, see Anavitarte, *El cacicazgo*.

III. SOME FURTHER RULES OF SUBSTANTIVE LAW

1. See for example: Levillier ed., *Gobernantes del Perú*, IX, 273–75; Murúa, *Historia del origen*, iii, xx, xxi, 211–13; Cobo, *Historia*, III, xii, xxvi, 238; Valera, *Las costumbres antiguas del*

Perú, p. 55 ff.; "Relación del origen é gobierno," in *Colección de libros y documentos*, p. 68; "El gobierno del Inga," in *Colección de libros y documentos*, p. 79; Acosta, *Natural and Moral History*, vi, xviii, 424; Castro and Ortega Morejón, "Relación," in Trimborn ed., *Quellen zur Kulturgeschichte*, p. 242.

2. Trimborn, "Straftat und Sühne in Alt-Peru," in *Zeitschrift für Ethnologie* (1925), p. 194; Trimborn, "Der Rechtsbruch in den Hochkulturen Amerikas," in *Zeitschrift für Vergleichende Rechtswissenschaft*, LI, 8–129.

3. Castro and Ortega Morejón, "Relación," in Trimborn ed., *Quellen zur Kulturgeschichte*, p. 242.

4. Cabello, *Miscelánea Antártica*, xx, p. 360.

5. Cobo, *Historia*, III, xii, xxvi, 242.

6. Cobo, *Historia*, III, xii, xxvi, 239; Acosta, *Natural and Moral History*, vi, xviii, 424.

7. Cobo, *Historia*, III, xii, xxvi, 242.

8. Rowe, "Inca Culture," in *Handbook of South American Indians*, II, 271; Cunow, *Die Soziale Verfassung des Inka-reichs*, p. 165; Baudin, *L'Empire socialiste des Inka*, p. 184; Trimborn, "Straftat und Sühne in Alt-Peru," in *Zeitschrift für Ethnologie* (1925), p. 223.

9. *Relaciones geográficas*, I, Rucanas Antamarcas, 207.

10. See Chap. IV of this book.

11. Garcilaso, *Royal Commentaries of the Yncas*, I, 147, says there was no discretion. I rely on Castro and Ortega Morejón who say the opposite, ("Relación," in Trimborn ed., *Quellen zur Kulturgeschichte*, p. 242), and on Santillán ("Relación," in Jiménez ed., *Tres Relaciones*, §§ 12, 13), who also says that judges had discretion, and I also rely on the fact that the Inca had no mechanical means of recording laws exactly.

12. Rowe, "Inca Culture," in *Handbook of South American Indians*, II, 271, describes the punishments succinctly: "The usual punishments were public rebuke, the HIWAYA, exile to the coca plantations, loss of office, torture and death. The HIWAYA consisted in dropping a stone on a man's back from a height of nearly 3 feet, often killing him. Death was inflicted by stoning, hanging by the feet, throwing from a cliff, or simply beating the head in with a club." Imprisonment was used for temporary custody, or as a sort of trial by ordeal or execution in which the accused was incarcerated with wild animals.

13. Cobo, *Historia,* III, xii, xxvi, 238.

14. Polo, "Relación," in *Colección de documentos inéditos,* XVII, 107.

15. Garcilaso, *Royal Commentaries of the Yncas,* I, 146.

16. Garcilaso, *Royal Commentaries of the Yncas,* I, 48.

17. "Horden que el Ynga tubo en la governación," (unpublished MS, British Museum, Fol. 413); Levillier ed., *Gobernantes del Perú,* IX, 276.

18. Poma, *Primer nueva corónica,* p. 187; Cobo, *Historia,* III, xii, xxvi, 239; De las Casas, *De las antiguas gentes del Perú,* p. 25.

19. Cobo, *Historia,* III, xii, xxvi, 241; see also Levillier ed., *Gobernantes del Perú,* IX, 275.

20. Levillier ed., *Gobernantes del Perú,* IX, 276; Cobo, *Historia,* III, 240.

21. Levillier ed., *Gobernantes del Perú,* IX, 274.

22. Levillier ed., *Gobernantes del Perú,* IX, 275.

23. Poma, *Primer nueva corónica,* p. 314; De las Casas, *De las antiguas gentes del Perú,* p. 212.

24. Levillier ed., *Gobernantes del Perú,* IX, 273. See also Cobo, *Historia,* III, xii, xxvi, 238.

25. See Appendix of this book.

26. Valera, *Las costumbres antiguas del Perú,* pp. 57–58.

27. Cobo, *Historia,* III, xii, xxvi, 242.

28. Cobo, *Historia,* III, xii, xxvi, 238; Levillier ed., *Gobernantes del Perú,* IX, 273.

29. See pp. 115, 116, 118 in this book.

30. Shades of the felony-murder rule.

31. This is from Levillier ed., *Gobernantes del Perú,* IX, 273; Cobo speaks only of exile.

32. Cobo, *Historia,* III, xii, xxvi, 237–38; Levillier ed., *Gobernantes del Perú,* IX, 273.

33. "El gobierno del Inga," in *Colección de libros y documentos,* p. 79; Valera, *Las costumbres antiguas del Perú,* pp. 8–11; Garcilaso denies that there was human sacrifice, but demonstrates his capacity for bland inconsistency by describing retainer burial, Garcilaso, *Royal Commentaries of the Yncas,* II, 113; Trimborn, "Straftat und Sühne," in *Zeitschrift für Ethnologie,* (1925), p. 235.

34. Cieza, *Crónica del Perú,* II, xxviii, 100, 109, 111, 113; Cieza, *Travels,* pp. 151, 180, 188, 203, 206, 223, 229, 311, 330, 355; De las Casas, *De las antiguas gentes del Perú,* p. 91; Acosta, *Natural and Moral History,* V, vii, 19, 313; Borregán, *Crónica,* p. 79; *Relaciones*

geográficas, III, Chunchi, 189; Murúa, *Historia del origen,* III, XL, 257, 291, 333; Molina, in Markham ed., *The Rites and Laws of the Yncas,* pp. 54–59; Cobo, *Historia,* III, XII, xxxix, 274, 277; Montesinos, "Memorias," in *Colección de libros y documentos,* pp. 41, 48; Roman y Zamora, *Republicas de indias,* pp. 225, 226; Matienzo, *Gobierno del Perú,* p. 12.

35. Rowe, "Inca Culture," in *Handbook of South American Indians,* II, 305.

36. Murúa, *Historia del origen,* III, lxi, 316–17; XIII, 94; "Relación . . . hecha por los primeros religiosos Agustinos," in *Colección de documentos inéditos,* III, 44; Molina, in Markham ed., *Rites and Laws of the Yncas,* p. 15; Garcilaso, *Royal Commentaries of the Yncas,* I, 148; Valera, *Las costumbres antiguas del Perú,* pp. 27–30; Calancha, "Corónica moralizada," in Riva Agüero ed., *Los cronistas de convento,* Series 1, No. 4, pp. 88–89.

37. "Relación del origen é gobierno," in *Colección de libros y documentos,* p. 69; Castro and Ortega Morejón, "Relación," in Trimborn ed., *Quellen zur Kulturgeschichte,* p. 242.

38. Castro and Ortega Morejón, "Relación," in Trimborn ed., *Quellen zur Kulturgeschichte,* p. 242; "Relación del origen é gobierno," in *Colección de libros y documentos,* pp. 74–75.

39. For the suspected crime of rebellion: Cieza, *Crónica del Perú,* II, p. 93.

40. Castro and Ortega Morejón, "Relación," in Trimborn ed., *Quellen zur Kulturgeschichte,* p. 240.

41. These were young girls, the "chosen women," ultimately to be allocated to the Inca or the Sun.

42. See pp. 119, 120 in this book.

43. Rowe, "Inca Culture," in *Handbook of South American Indians,* II, 271.

44. Castro and Ortega Morejón, "Relación," in Trimborn ed., *Quellen zur Kulturgeschichte,* p. 242.

45. Valera, *Las costumbres antiguas del Perú,* pp. 57–58.

46. Cobo, *Historia,* III, XII, xxvi, 240.

47. Levillier ed., *Gobernantes del Perú,* IX, 274.

48. See Appendix of this book.

49. Poma, *Primer nueva corónica,* p. 187.

50. Hoebel, *The Law of Primitive Man,* p. 293.

51. Hoebel, *The Law of Primitive Man,* p. 329.

52. Rowe, "Inca Culture," in *Handbook of South American Indians,* II, 270; Means, *Ancient Civilizations of the Andes,* pp. 313–17;

Valcárcel, "Indian Markets and Fairs in Peru," in *Handbook of South American Indians*, II, 477; Murra, his dissertation contains an excellent and exhaustive discussion of the evidence.

53. Rowe, "Inca Culture," in *Handbook of South American Indians*, II, 270.

54. Cieza, *Travels*, p. 390; De las Casas, *De las antiguas gentes del Perú*, p. 49; Borregán, *Crónica*, p. 81.

55. Cabello, *Miscelánea Antártica*, III, xix, p. 349; Valera, *Las costumbres antiguas del Perú*, p. 82.

56. Merchants are occasionally mentioned. Cabello, *Miscelánea Antártica*, III, xix, 349. For other references see Murra, "The Economic Organization of the Inca State," (unpublished MS, University of Chicago).

57. Cieza, *Travels*, p. 361.

58. Castro and Ortega Morejón, "Relación," in Trimborn ed., *Quellen zur Kulturgeschichte*, pp. 245–46.

59. Rowe, "Inca Culture," in *Handbook of South American Indians*, II, 270; see also Means, *Ancient Civilizations of the Andes*, pp. 323–25.

60. De las Casas, *De las antiguas gentes del Perú*, pp. 213, 233; "Relación del origen é gobierno," in *Colección de libros y documentos*, p. 65; Levillier ed., *Gobernantes del Perú*, I, 290 and 291.

61. *Relaciones geográficas*, II, Provincia de las Pascajes, 63, and III, Quito y su distrito, 45, 98; Cobo, *Historia*, III, xi, viii, 43–44.

62. *Relaciones geográficas*, III, Quito y su distrito, 98.

63. Acosta, *Natural and Moral History*, IV, iii, 189.

64. Acosta, *Natural and Moral History*, IV, xxii, 246.

65. See p. 29 in this book.

66. See references cited in the rest of this section.

67. Letter to Toledo in *Colección de libros y documentos*, VI, Series 2, 200–3.

68. Levillier ed., *Don Francisco de Toledo*, II, 3–13.

69. Valera, *Las costumbres antiguas del Perú*, p. 117, states that many laws of the provinces were left as they were before the Inca conquest, and that many were changed. The inheritance of estates, and succession to official positions, was approved according to the ancient custom of each province. Garcilaso, *Royal Commentaries of the Yncas*, I, 312, says substantially the same.

70. See for example Cabello, *Miscelánea Antártica*, xv, 304, describing the Chanca wars in which the Inca killed the Chanca leaders, but placed their sons in office; see Rowe, "Kingdom of Chimor," in *Acta Americana*, VI.

71. See list in Castro and Ortega Morejón, "Relación," in Trimborn ed., *Quellen zur Kulturgeschichte,* p. 243. See also Trimborn, "Familien und Erbrecht," in *Zeitschrift für Vergleichende Rechtswissenschaft,* pp. 42, 352–92.

72. See Cobo, *Historia,* III, xii, xxvii, 243–46; Valera, *Las costumbres antiguas del Perú,* 108–12.

73. See for example: Cieza, *Crónica del Perú,* II, xix, 73; Valera, *Las costumbres antiguas del Perú,* p. 114; De las Casas, *De las antiguas gentes del Perú,* p. 158; Poma, *Primer nueva corónica,* p. 187; Montestinos, "Memorias," in *Colección de libros y documentos,* p. 36; Murúa, *Historia del origen,* p. 171.

74. See Appendix of this book.

75. See pp. 27–37, 93–98 in this book.

76. Cobo, *Historia,* III, xii, xxvi, 234–36; Falcón, "Relación," in *Colección de libros y documentos,* XI, Series 1, 146.

77. Castro and Ortega Morejón, "Relación," in Trimborn ed., *Quellen zur Kulturgeschichte,* p. 243.

78. Murúa, *Historia del origen,* III, vi, 175; Baudin, *L'Empire socialiste des Inca,* p. 67, also cites Santillán, "Relación," Para. 18; Castro and Ortega Morejón, "Relación," in Trimborn ed., *Quellen zur Kulturgeschichte,* p. 243; though Cobo, *Historia,* III, xii, xxxvi, 284, speaks of the 1st born son.

79. Acosta, *Natural and Moral History,* VI, xii, pp. 411–12.

80. Murúa, *Historia del origen,* III, vi, 175.

81. See Rowe, "Inca Culture," in *Handbook of South American Indians,* II, 208–9; Gibson, "The Inca Concept of Sovereignty," in *University of Texas Latin-American Studies,* IV.

82. Sancho, "Relación," in *Los cronistas de la conquista,* p. 179; Acosta, *Natural and Moral History,* V, v, 312; Cieza, *Crónica del Perú,* II, 37; Castro and Ortega Morejón, "Relación," in Trimborn ed., *Quellen zur Kulturgeschichte,* p. 239; Cobo, *Historia,* III, xii, xxxvi, 290; Polo, "Relación," in *Colección de documentos inéditos,* XVII, lxix, 96.

83. Castro and Ortega Morejón, "Relación," in Trimborn ed., *Quellen zur Kulturgeschichte,* pp. 239, 245.

84. See also Acosta, *Natural and Moral History,* V, v, 312.

85. Cieza, *Crónica del Perú,* II, 37; Sancho, "Relación," in *Los cronistas de la conquista,* p. 179.

86. Cieza, *Crónica del Perú,* II, x, 32–34.

87. Cobo, *Historia,* III, xii, xxv, 234; see also Falcón, "Relación," in *Colección de libros ye documentos,* Vol. XI, Series 1, 146.

88. Cabello, *Miscelánea Antártica,* p. 348

89. Cobo, *Historia*, III, xii, xxv, 235.

90. Falcón, "Relación," in *Colección de libros y documentos,* XI, Series 1, 146–47.

91. *Relaciones geográficas*, III, Loxa, 217.

92. Acosta, *Natural and Moral History*, VI, xii, 411–12.

93. Cieza, *Travels*, pp. 151, 161–62, 181.

94. To the same effect, *Relaciones geográficas*, II, Piura, 240.

95. *Relaciones geográficas*, I, Guamanga, 101.

96. Castro and Ortega Morejón, "Relación," in Trimborn ed., *Quellen zur Kulturgeschichte*, p. 243.

97. Santillán, "Relación," in Jiménez ed., *Tres relaciones,* pp. 24–27.

98. De las Casas, *De las antiguas gentes del Perú*, p. 109.

99. De las Casas, *De las antiguas gentes del Perú*, p. 111.

100. Cieza, *Travels*, p. 181.

101. *Relaciones geográficas*, II, La Paz, 72.

102. Garcilaso, *Royal Commentaries of the Yncas*, I, 310–12.

103. Rowe, "Inca Culture," in *Handbook of South American Indians*, II, 254.

104. *Relaciones geográficas*, I, Guamanga, 100.

105. *Relaciones geográficas*, I, Guamanga, 100.

106. To the same effect: Polo, "Relación," in *Colección de documentos inéditos*, XVII, 58; Santillán, "Relación," in Jiménez ed., *Tres relaciones*, p. 24; Castro and Ortega Morejón, "Relación," in Trimborn ed., *Quellen zur Kulturgeschichte*, p. 244; Lizarraga, in Riva Agüero ed., *Los cronistas de convento*, pp. 157–58.

107. Cobo, *Historia*, III, xii, xxviii, 250.

108. Castro and Ortega Morejón, "Relación," in Trimborn ed., *Quellen zur Kulturgeschichte*, p. 243; Santillán, "Relación," Jiménez ed., *Tres relaciones*, pp. 24–27.

109. Castro and Ortega Morejón, "Relación," in Trimborn ed., *Quellen zur Kulturgeschichte*, p. 244.

IV. THE POLITICAL SYSTEM AND ITS JUDICIAL FUNCTIONS

1. Urteaga, "La organización judicial," in *Revista histórica de Lima*, IX, opposite p. 28.

2. See for example Means, *Ancient Civilizations of the Andes*, p. 292.

3. See pp. 27–37, 93–98 in this book.

4. Cobo, *Historia*, III, xⅡ, xxv, 235; Cieza, *Travels*, pp. 150–53.

5. Cieza, *Travels*, pp. 164–65; "Relación del origen é gobierno," in *Colección de libros y documentos*, p. 71.

6. Cobo, *Historia*, III, xⅡ, xxv, 229.

7. Cieza, *Crónica del Perú*, II, xⅨ, 71; Borregán, *Crónica*, p. 28.

8. Cieza, *Crónica del Perú*, II, xⅢ, xⅣ, xⅦ, xxⅣ.

9. Cieza, *Travels*, pp. 278, 311.

10. Levillier ed., *Gobernantes del Perú*, IX, 285; Cobo, *Historia*, III, xⅡ, xxiii, 222.

11. Polo, "Relación," in *Colección de documentos inéditos*, XVII, 105; Baudin, *L'Empire socialiste des Inka*, pp. 62, 182; Cobo, *Historia*, III, xⅡ, xxii, 218; Cieza, *Travels*, p. 330.

12. Cieza, *Crónica del Perú*, II, 62.

13. Cobo, *Historia*, III, xⅡ, xxii, 224; xxv, 234; Cabello, *Miscelánea Antártica*, xvi, 320; xviii, 339–40; xxi, 362; xxvii, 425.

14. Cieza, *Travels*, pp. 149–50; Cieza, *Crónica del Perú*, II, xⅢ, pp. 44–45; *Relaciones geográficas*, II, Abancay, 208; Cobo, *Historia*, III, xⅡ, xxiv, 224.

15. "Declaración . . . a Vaca de Castro," in *Colección de libros y documentos*, III, Series 2, 16.

16. Cobo, *Historia*, III, xⅡ, xxvi, 240.

17. Rowe has called it a "colonization program" and asserts that resettlement took place on a vast scale, "Inca Culture," in *Handbook of South American Indians*, II, 269.

18. Cobo, *Historia*, III, xⅡ, xxiii, 223.

19. *Relaciones geográficas*, III, Sant Andres Xunxi, 151.

20. Polo, "Relación," in *Colección de documentos inéditos*, XVII, 105.

21. "Relación . . . hecha por los primeros religiosos Agustinos," in *Colección de documentos inéditos*, III, 31.

22. Montesinos, "Memorias," in *Colección de libros y documentos*, XVI, Series 2, 36; Acosta, *Natural and Moral History*, VI, xvi, 422; De las Casas, *De las antiguas gentes del Perú*, pp. 173–74; Cobo, *Historia*, III, xⅡ, xxiv, 230.

23. Cobo, *Historia*, III, xⅡ, xxvi, 240–41.

24. Poma, *Primer nueva corónica*, p. 192.

25. Cieza, *Travels*, p. 150; Cobo, *Historia*, III, xⅡ, xxiii, 223; Poma, *Primer nueva corónica*, p. 195; Cabello, *Miscelánea Antártica*, xviii, 340.

26. Cobo, *Historia*, III, xⅡ, xxiii, 224; see also Poma, *Primer nueva corónica*, p. 189, who says *mitimaes* were given two wives.

27. Cieza, *Crónica del Perú*, II, xxii, 86.

28. "Relación . . . hecha por los primeros religiosos Agustinos," in *Colección de documentos inéditos*, III, 31.

29. Cobo, *Historia*, III, xii, xxiii, 222; *Relaciones geográficas*, III, Cuenca, 171.

30. "Declaración . . . a Vaca de Castro," in *Colección de libros y documentos*, III, Series 2, 18–19.

31. There appear to have been some purely military border garrisons (Cieza, *Crónica del Perú*, II, xxii, 87–88). There were also settlements of people called *mitimaes* established a distance from some highland home villages in order to cultivate crops in the valleys which could not be grown in the native climate. Cobo (*Historia*, III, xii, xxiii, 226), says this was true of the whole province of Collao. See also Polo, "Relación," in *Colección de documentos inéditos*, XVII, 45. Close connections were maintained with the native village, and the valley settlement remained under the administrative control of the ruler of the native village, and all produce was brought home.

32. Cieza, *Travels*, p. 149.

33. Levillier, ed., *Gobernantes del Perú*, I, 296.

34. Cobo, *Historia*, III, xii, xxxv, 278–79; "El gobierno del Inga" in *Colección de libros y documentos*, III, Series 2, 78–79.

35. See pp. 93–98 in this book.

36. Murúa, *Historia del origen*, iii, vi, 175; Gibson, "The Inca Concept of Sovereignty," in *University of Texas Latin American Studies*, IV.

37. See discussions by Baudin, *L'Empire socialiste des Inka*, p. 66; Gibson, "The Inca Concept of Sovereignty," in *University of Texas Latin American Studies*, pp. 54–55.

38. Murúa, *Historia del origen*, III, xxi, 213–15.

39. Post-runners were continuously on duty at intervals on the royal roads.

40. Cobo, *Historia*, III, xii, xxxv, 279.

41. Cobo, *Historia*, III, xii, xxx, 257.

42. Cobo, *Historia*, III, xii, xxxiii, 272 and 274.

43. Polo, "Relación," in *Colección documentos inéditos*, XVII, 68–69.

44. Castro and Ortega Morejón, "Relación," in Trimborn ed., *Quellen zur Kulturgeschichte*, p. 244; Cobo, *Historia*, III, xii, xxi, 255.

45. Polo, "Relación," in *Colección de documentos inéditos*, XVII, 33.

46. Castro and Ortega Morejón, "Relación," in Trimborn ed., *Quellen zur Kulturgeschichte*, pp. 244 and 245; Cobo, *Historia*, III, 246.

47. Cieza, *Crónica del Perú*, II, xix, 71; Cobo, *Historia*, III, 227–29, 258; Valera, *Las costumbres antiguas del Perú*, pp. 110–11.

48. Cobo, *Historia*, III, xii, xxxiii, 269–74.

49. Polo, "Relación," in *Colección de documentos inéditos*, XVII, 27–28.

50. Cobo, *Historia*, III, xii, xxxi, 255.

51. See discussion of *mitimaes* earlier in this section.

52. Cieza, *Crónica del Perú*, II, xxi, 79; Cobo, *Historia*, III, xii, xxxiii, 267–68; Polo, "Relación," in *Colección de documentos inéditos*, XVII, 73.

53. Castro and Ortega Morejón, "Relación," in Trimborn ed., *Quellen zur Kulturgeschichte*, p. 226.

54. Cobo, *Historia*, III, xii, xxv, 232.

55. Cobo, *Historia*, III, xii, xxv, 233; Santillán "Relación," in Jiménez ed., *Tres relaciones*, p. 17.

56. Murúa, *Historia del origen*, iii, vi, 164, 167, 177–78.

57. Molina, "Fables and Rites of the Yncas" in Markham ed., *The Rites and Laws of the Yncas*, pp. 13–14.

58. There were eleven royal *ayllus*, yet Urteaga's tribunal is composed of twelve judges. These royal *ayllus* and the other *ayllus* in the neighborhood of Cuzco were grouped into two divisions, usually called "moieties" in the literature. These were called "Hanan-saya" or Upper division, and "Hurin-saya" or Lower division. (Cobo, *Historia*, III, 229). Within the provinces of the rest of the empire the Inca government instituted analogous subgroupings (Castro and Ortega Morejón, "Relación," in Trimborn ed., *Quellen zur Kulturgeschichte*, p. 237; Cobo, *Historia*, III, 229–30), which probably corresponded to the group governed by the *hunu* immediately beneath governor in the decimal system. Rowe ("Inca Culture," in *Handbook of South American Indians*, II, 263) has cited evidence from the *Relaciones geográficas* that the dual division did not always apply in the provinces and that there were sometimes three. The Hanan and Hurin moiety division appears to have had ceremonial and competitive significance rather than any fundamental political importance.

59. "Relación del origen é gobierno," in *Colección de libros y documentos*, p. 72; *Relaciones geográficas*, I, Guamanga, 100.

60. Castro and Ortega Morejón, "Relación," in Trimborn ed., *Quellen zur Kulturgeschichte*, p. 242.

61. "Relación del origen é gobierno," in *Colección de libros y documentos*, p. 65; Cobo, *Historia*, III, xii, xxiv, 229.

62. Castro and Ortega Morejón, "Relación," in Trimborn ed., *Quellen zur Kulturgeschichte*, p. 241.

63. Levillier, ed., *Gobernantes del Perú*, IX, 282–87; "Relación del origen é gobierno," in *Colección de libros y documentos*, pp. 68–69; Castro and Ortega Morejón, "Relación," in Trimborn ed., *Quellen zur Kulturgeschichte*, p. 242.

64. Castro and Ortega Morejón, "Relación," in Trimborn ed., *Quellen zur Kulturgeschichte*, p. 245.

65. Cieza, *Crónica del Perú*, II, xviii.

66. Castro and Ortega Morejón, "Relación," in Trimborn, ed., *Quellen zur Kulturgeschichte*, p. 242.

67. Santillán, "Relación," in Jiménez ed., *Tres relaciones*, p. 23.

68. Cobo, *Historia*, III, xii, xxvi, 237; Cieza, *Crónica del Perú*, XX, 78.

69. Cieza, *Travels*, p. 153.

70. Cobo, *Historia*, III, xii, xxv, 236.

71. Cobo, *Historia*, III, xii, xxv, 235.

72. Cieza, *Crónica del Perú*, II, xii, 33.

73. Cieza, *Travels*, p. 153; "Relación del origen é gobierno," in *Colección de libros y documentos*, pp. 68–69.

74. *Relaciones geográficas*, I, Guamanga, 99; "Horden que el Ynga tubo en la governación," (unpublished MS, British Museum, Fol. 413).

75. "Relación del origen é gobierno," in *Colección de libros y documentos*, p. 47.

76. Cobo, *Historia*, III, xii, xxv, 235.

77. Rowe, "Inca Culture," in *Handbook of South American Indians*, II, 264. I have adopted Rowe's phonetic spelling of *t'oqrikoq* and *tokoyrikoq* because of the confusion mentioned. Names of other officials have been spelled in the erratic hispanicized manner of the chroniclers.

78. In support of this view see Falcón, "Relación," in *Colección de libros y documentos*, XI, Series 1, 147.

79. Cobo, *Historia*, III, xii, xxv, 232–36; Polo, "Report," in Markham ed., *Rites and Laws of the Yncas*, p. 155.

80. Cobo, *Historia*, III, xii, xxv, 233.

81. Levillier ed., *Gobernantes del Perú*, IX, 272.

82. Santillán, "Relación," in Jiménez ed., *Tres relaciones*, pp. 18–19.

83. Cobo, *Historia*, III, xii, xxv, 234.

84. Montesinos, "Memorias," in *Colección de libros y documentos*, p. 34, says that even the "tukrikuk's" power was limited, and that in important matters and those cases involving the death penalty the King gave sentence. This may be just one of Montesinos' many unreliable moments.

85. "Relación del origen é gobierno," in *Colección de libros y documentos*, p. 74; "Horden que el Ynga tubo en la governación," (unpublished MS, British Museum, Fol. 413).

86. Cobo, *Historia*, III, xii, xvi, 238.

87. Cobo, *Historia*, III, xii, xxv, 236.

88. Cobo, *Historia*, III, xii, xxvi, 241; Levillier ed., *Gobernantes del Perú*, IX, 274.

89. Cobo, *Historia*, III, xii, xxv, 235; Montesinos, "Memorias," in *Colección de libros y documentos*, p. 34.

90. Cobo, *Historia*, III, xii, xxv, pp. 232–37.

91. Levillier ed., *Gobernantes del Perú*, IX, 283.

92. Levillier ed., *Gobernantes del Perú*, IX, 284–85.

93. Levillier ed., *Gobernantes del Perú*, IX, 277 and 283; Garcilaso, *Royal Commentaries of the Yncas*, I, 149.

94. See Valera, *Las costumbres antiguas del Perú*, p. 117, where he says many laws were left as they were.

95. See Appendix of this book.

96. Levillier ed., *Gobernantes del Perú*, IX, 275.

97. See pp. 115, 116 in this book.

98. Cieza, *Crónica del Perú*, II, xxix, 117, says *"capaccocha . . . era oprenda que se pagaba en lugar de diezmo á los templos."*

99. Castro and Ortega Morejón, "Relación," in Trimborn ed., *Quellen zur Kulturgeschichte*, p. 240.

100. Castro and Ortega Morejón, "Relación," in Trimborn ed., *Quellen zur Kulturgeschichte*, p. 241.

101. Santillán, "Relación," in Jiménez ed., *Tres relaciones*, p. 23.

102. Valera, *Las costumbres antiguas del Perú*, pp. 19–25, 32.

103. Garcilaso, *Royal Commentaries of the Yncas*, I, 150–51.

104. Santillán, "Relación," in Jiménez ed., *Tres relaciones*, pp. 18–19.

105. *Relaciones geográficas* I, Guamanga, 101.

106. See Holguín, *Vocabulario*, II, 182–83, for list of words relating to judiciary.

107. Cobo, *Historia*, III, xii, xxvi, 237; "Relación del origen é gobierno," in *Colección de libros y documentos*, p. 74.

108. "Horden que el Ynga tubo en la governación" (unpublished MS, British Museum, Fol. 413). See also Levillier ed., *Gobernantes del Perú*, IX, 276.

109. "Relación del origen é gobierno," in *Colección de libros y documentos*, p. 74; "Horden que el Ynga tubo en la governación" (unpublished MS, British Museum, Fol. 413); Cobo, *Historia*, III, xii, xxv, 237; Levillier ed., *Gobernantes del Perú*, IX, 272 and 276.

110. "Relación del origen é gobierno," in *Colleción de libros y documentos*, p. 69; Castro and Ortega Morejón, "Relación," in Trimborn ed., *Quellen zur Kulturgeschichte*, p. 242; Cieza, *Crónica del Perú*, p. 93.

111. Levillier ed., *Gobernantes del Perú*, IX, 272 and 282.

112. Rowe, "Kingdom of Chimor," in *Acta Americana*, VI, 46.

113. Robert H. Lowie, *The Origin of the State* (Harcourt Brace and Co., New York, 1927), pp. 16–17.

114. West African Kingdom described in R. S. Rattray *Ashanti Law and Constitution*, (Oxford, 1929).

115. Hoebel, *The Law of Primitive Man*, p. 212.

116. Cultural differences having political significance are intended to be stressed here rather than differences in basic level of development.

117. Betanzos "Suma y narración," *Biblioteca Hispano-Ultramarina*, X, 60–62; XIII, 81; XVI, 108; Morúa, *Historia de los Incas*, iii, xlviii, 225.

118. See citations of Baudin in *L'Empire socialiste des Inka*, p. 66.

119. Rowe, "Inca Culture," in *Handbook of South American Indians*, II, 183.

V. INCA LAW, THEORY AND PRACTICE

1. See A. R. Radcliffe-Brown, Roscoe Pound in *The Encyclopedia of Social Sciences* (N.Y., 1933), under Law. E. Adamson Hoebel's similar definition in *The Law of Primitive Man*, p. 28 is: "A social norm is legal if its neglect or infraction is regularly met, in threat or in fact, by application of physical force by an individual or a group possessing the socially recognized privilege of so acting."

2. Stone, quoted in Hoebel, *The Law of Primitive Man*, p. 16.

3. Hoebel, *The Law of Primitive Man,* p. 143.

4. Hoebel, *The Law of Primitive Man,* p. 191.

5. Harold Lasswell, *World Politics and Personal Insecurity* (New York, 1935), p. 29.

6. Milovan Djilas, *The New Class* (London, 1957), p. 59.

7. Robert Redfield, *The Primitive World and Its Transformations,* Ithaca, 1953, p. 112.

8. T. S. Eliot, *Notes Towards the Definition of Culture* (New York, 1949).

• APPENDIX: FORBIDDEN ACTS
AND THEIR PENALTIES

Most of the fragments in the chronicles which allude to punishable offenses are brief to the point of inadequacy. They must generally be looked upon with considerable reservations. The following lists give most of the commonly cited bits and pieces which the Spaniards recorded, but no claim is made to absolute completeness.

BREACH OF RULE AFFECTING INCA OR CASTE PROPERTY OR RIGHTS

Hunting where forbidden
  1st time   Punished [a]
  2d time   Tortured [a]
  3rd time   Death [a]
Hunting without permission
  1st time   Stone punishment [b]
  2d time   Death [b]
Hunting in Inca preserve   Death [c]
Taking gold and silver out of
  Cuzco   Death [d]; no penalty mentioned [e]
Intercourse with women of Inca
  or Sun   Death [f]
Breaking into house of mama-
  conas   Death hanging by feet [g]
Theft of Inca or Sun property
  however small   Death [h]
Wearing of sumptuary articles   No penalty mentioned [i]

[a] Levillier ed., *Gobernantes del Perú,* IX, 275, 285.
[b] Cobo, *Historia,* III, xii, xxvi, 241.   [c] Cieza, *Travels,* p. 288.
[d] Cieza, *Travels,* p. 329.   [e] Cobo, *Historia,* III, xii, xxv, 291.
[f] "Relación del origen é gobierno," p. 68; Santillán, *Relación,* p. 22; Acosta, *Natural and Moral History,* v, xv, 333.
[g] Levillier ed., *Gobernantes del Perú,* IX, 276.
[h] Levillier ed., *Gobernantes del Perú,* IX, 274.
[i] Cieza, *Crónica del Perú,* ii, xix, 73; Valera, *Las costumbres antiguas del Perú,* p. 114; De las Casas, *De las antiguas del Perú,* p. 158.

BREACH OF RULE AFFECTING GOVERNMENT

Disobedience in tribute	Severe punishment and increased tax [a]
Failure to do job properly: craftsmen, herders	Public punishment, blows with stone or whip [b]
Concealment of person from census taker	Blows with stone [c]
Bribery of annual inspectors	Severe punishment for both briber and official [d]
Acceptance of bribe or robbery of pueblo by inspector	Severe punishment; deprived of office and sent to mines or to carry wood in temples [e]
Moving boundary markers	
1st time	Torture [f]
2d time	Death [b,f]
Rebellion	Deprived of estates; town punished, ringleaders sent to Cuzco as prisoners [g]
Treason	Death [p]
Disobeying curaca	Death [h]
1st time	Discretionary [n]
2d time	Stone punishment [n]
3rd time	Death [n]
1st time	Torture [i]
if continues	Exile or death [i]
Disrespect toward administrators	Severe punishment [m]
Fleeing town of residence when had job obligation	Death [h]
if man	Blows with stone until dead [j]
if woman without children	Hanged [j]
if woman has children	Other punishment [j]
if *mitimae*	Death [j]
1st time	Torture [k]
2d time	Death [k]
if person in army	Death [h]
if person in Inca service	Death [j]
Not wearing proper distinctive costume indicating locality of origin	Severe punishment, 100 blows, or death [l]

Traveling without permission	Severe punishment [o]
Moving residence	Illegal [q]
Failing in service to *tambo*	*Cacique* in charge of *tambo* punished [r]
Failure of cacique:	
to punish or to report crimes of his pueblos	Deprived of office [s]
to report punishment administered	Deprived of office and punished; death if a serious matter [s]
to be just	Blows or death: Inca judged *hunus* and above; governors and inspectors judged officials below [t]
to obtain authority before imposing death penalty	Blows with a stone or death, according to the crime punished [u]
to perform obligation of eating in public in the plaza with his Indians	Removal from office [s]
Laesae majestatis by priest	Deprived of job and estate and sent to mines [v]

[a] Cieza, *Crónica del Perú*, ii, xviii, 70.

[b] Murúa, *Historia del origen*, iii, xx, 211.

[c] Castro and Ortega Morejón, *Relación*, p. 241.

[d] "Relación del origen é gobierno," p. 68.

[e] Valera, *Las costumbres antiguas del Perú*, p. 23.

[f] Levillier ed., *Gobernantes del Perú*, IX, 275; Cobo, *Historia*, III, xii, xxxvi, 241.

[g] Cieza, *Crónica del Perú*, ii, xiii, 45; lxi, 233.

[h] "Relación del origen é gobierno," p. 68; Murúa, *Historia del origen*, iii, xx, 211.

[i] Levillier ed., *Gobernantes del Perú*, IX, 274.

[j] Murúa, *Historia del origen*, iii, xx, 211.   [k] Santillán, *Relación*, p. 22.

[l] Levillier ed., *Gobernantes del Perú*, IX, 276, 285; Poma, *Primer nueva corónica*, p. 192; Cobo, *Historia*, III, xii, xvi, 240–41.

[m] Levillier ed., *Gobernantes del Perú*, IX, 275; imprisonment or if combined with other crime, death, according to Cobo, *Historia*, III, xii, xxvi, 241.

[n] Cobo, *Historia*, III, xii, xxvi, 240.

[o] De las Casas, *De las antiguas gentes del Perú*, p. 184.

[p] Poma, *Primer nueva corónica*, pp. 187, 314.

[q] Garcilaso, *Royal Commentaries of the Yncas*, I, 308.

[r] Levillier ed., *Gobernantes del Perú*, IX, 275; Cobo, *Historia*, III, xii, xxvi, 241.

[s] Levillier ed., *Gobernantes del Perú*, IX, 275.

[t] Murúa, *Historia del origen*, iii, xxi, 213.

[u] Cobo, *Historia*, III, xii, xxvi, 238.

[v] Valera, *Las costumbres antiguas del Perú*, p. 32.

HOMICIDE

Treasonable killing, whether condemned is nobleman or commoner	Death [a] [b]
Homicide by witchcraft	Death to killer and his family in order that knowledge of witchcraft perish; [a] [b] death [b]
Abortion by blows, magic or herbs	Death [d]
Homicide in family	
man kills wife for adultery	No penalty [a] [b]
man kills wife for other reasons:	
if noble	As Inca saw fit, short of death [a]
if commoner	Death [a] [b]
Killing to rob	Torture and death [a] [b]
Killing in a quarrel	
if instigator is victim	Exile [b]
if instigator is killer	Discretionary with Inca; [a] death or exile to coca plantations [a] [b]
Cacique kills subject without permission	
1st offense	Stone punishment [a]
2d offense	Death, sometimes commuted to exile [a] [b]
Unjustified homicide	Death [e]

[a] Cobo, *Historia*, III, xii, xxvi, 238.
[b] Levillier ed., *Gobernantes del Perú*, IX, 273.
[c] Poma, *Primer nueva corónica*, p. 187.
[d] Levillier ed., *Gobernantes del Perú*, IX, 273; Valera, *Las costumbres antiguas del Perú*, p. 57; Cobo, *Historia*, III, xii, xxvi, 239.
[e] Acosta, *Natural and Moral History*, vi, xviii, 424; Poma, *Primer nueva corónica*, p. 314; Valera, *Las costumbres antiguas del Perú*, p. 57.

SEXUAL CRIMES

Incest
  ascendants or descendants of
    1st degree — Death [a]
  fornication in instances in
    which marriage was pro-
    hibited:
    if commoner — Death [b]
    if noble — Public reprimand [a b] [According to Acosta, Inca and nobles were permitted to marry their sisters.]

  avuncular relations ⎫ if woman
  cousins of 2d   ⎪ neither
    grade   ⎬ married
  affinals of 1st   ⎪ nor
    grade   ⎭ virgin — Beaten and shaved; men sent to mines, women to temple service [c]

  between father and daughter:
    where she was a virgin and
      consented — Death for both [c]
    where he forced daughter — Death for him; she sent to serve *acllas,* but could marry if anyone wanted her [c]

  between mother and son — Death for both [c d]
  between mother and daughter — 200 blows and exile [d]
  between brother and sister
    (same mother or father or
    half-sister):
    if virgin and consented — Death for both [c]
    if brother forced sister — He hanged; she sent to serve *acllas* [c]

Intercourse with women of Inca,
  sun, or huacas — Death [e f]
Rape
  1st time — Not death—unless with Inca's women [f]

  2d time — Death [f]

of virgin	Death by stoning [g]
unless she wishes to marry him in which case	Not death, only both beaten [g]
but if he is married and a father	He condemned; she sent to temple service [g]
of married woman	Death by hanging [g]
if virgin consented	Both beaten, hair shaved off, he exiled to mines, she to temple service; [g] death [h]
Seduction	
if virgin daughter of noble	Death [i]
if virgin daughter of commoner:	
1st time	Torture [i]
2d time	Death [i]
of unmarried woman	Death [i]
Polygamy [permitted according to rank]	No penalty mentioned for violation [j]
Pimps and bawds	Severe public punishment; death if continues [k]
Exogamy from pueblo	Punished [k]
Sodomy	Death and burning of body and all clothes [l]
Adultery or rape by priests, if women neither married nor virgins	
1st time	Deprived of office for a fixed time [m]
3rd time	Deprived of office for life [m]
Adultery	
commoner with wife of commoner	Torture [n]
commoner with wife of noble	Death [n]
wife and lover	Death, unless forgiven by husband—in that case lesser penalty; [o] death [p]
if woman forced man	Death for her; blows and exile for him [q]
if man forced woman	Death for him; 200 blows with rope, exile in service of acclla-conas for her [r]
of the husband or the wife	Death [m]

[a] Acosta, *Natural and Moral History*, vi, xviii, 424.
[b] Cobo, *Historia*, III, xii, xxvi, 239.
[c] Valera, *Las costumbres antiguas del Perú*, pp. 58–59.
[d] Poma, *Primer nueva corónica*, pp. 188, 190.
[e] Cobo, *Historia*, III, xii, xxvi, 239; Levillier ed., *Gobernantes del Perú*, IX, 282; Molina (Chile), *Las corónicas de los Molinas*, p. 21; Valera, *Las costumbres antiguas del Perú*, pp. 142–43; Cieza, *Crónica del Perú*, ii, xxvii; Acosta, *Natural and Moral History*, v, xv, 333; "Relación del origen é gobierno," p. 68.
[f] Levillier ed., *Gobernantes del Perú*, IX, 273.
[g] Valera, *Las costumbres antiguas del Perú*, p. 58.
[h] Poma, *Primer nueva corónica*, p. 188.
[i] Levillier ed., *Gobernantes del Perú*, IX, 274–75.
[j] Poma, *Primer nueva corónica*, p. 189.
[k] Levillier ed., *Gobernantes del Perú*, IX, 274, 275; Garcilaso, *Royal Commentaries of the Yncas*, I, 308.
[l] Valera, *Las costumbres antiguas del Perú*, p. 59; Garcilaso, *Royal Commentaries of the Yncas*, I, 245.
[m] Valera, *Las costumbres antiguas del Perú*, pp. 25, 58.
[n] Cobo, *Historia*, III, xii, xxvi, 239; Levillier ed., *Gobernantes del Perú*, IX, 274.
[o] Acosta, *Natural and Moral History*, vi, xviii, 424.
[p] Cieza, *Travels*, p. 363; Poma, *Primer nueva corónica*, p. 307; De las Casas, *De las antiguas gentes del Perú*, pp. 204, 211.
[q] Poma, *Primer nueva corónica*, p. 307.
[r] De las Casas, *De las antiguas gentes del Perú*, pp. 204, 211; Poma, *Primer nueva corónica*, p. 307.

THEFT

Theft of food	
when field did not belong to Inca:	
1st offense	Reprimand [a]
2d offense	Public punishment with stone [a]
when field belonged to Inca	Death [a]
because of poverty	Slight punishment [b]
because of necessity when traveling on road	No punishment [b]
out of vice	Torture [b]
by recidivist	Death [b]
Theft because of poverty	
thief was	Pardoned [c]
man in charge of thief was	Punished [c]
Theft out of vice	Repayment and exile [d]
if commoner	Hanged [e]
if noble	Death in prison [e]
Theft of minor object	
1st offense	Public blows [e]

2d offense	Torture [e]
3rd offense	Death [e]
Theft of important object	
1st offense	Death hanging by feet [e]
Theft of *any* Inca or Sun property	Death [b]
If travelers robbed in *tambo*, cacique in charge of service of *tambo* was	Punished [f] [g]
pueblo in charge of *tambo*	Was punished by *cacique;* [f] made good the theft and punished the culprit [g]
Theft by army passing through	Severe punishment, even death [h] [i]
Thievery	Death [k]
herder when animal unaccounted for [theft or negligence?]	Had to pay for missing animal [l]
thief	
1st offense	50 blows [j]
2d offense	Death [j]
finder [since caught thief might pose as one] who restores object	Not accused as thief [j]

[a] Cobo, *Historia,* III, xii, xxvi, 240.

[b] Murúa, *Historia del origen,* iii, xx, 211; Levillier ed., *Gobernantes del Perú,* IX, 274.

[c] Valera, *Las costumbres antiguas del Perú,* p. 59.

[d] Cobo, *Historia,* III, xii, xxvi, 239.

[e] Murúa, *Historia del origen,* iii, xx, 211.

[f] Cobo, *Historia,* III, xii, xxvi, 241.

[g] Levillier ed., *Gobernantes del Perú,* IX, 274.

[h] Cieza, *Crónica del Perú,* ii, xxiii, 93.

[i] De las Casas, *De las antiguas gentes del Perú,* p. 190.

[j] Poma, *Primer nueva corónica,* p. 187.

[k] Acosta, *Natural and Moral History,* vi, xviii, 424; *Relaciones geográficas,* I, 207.

[l] De las Casas, *De las antiguas gentes del Perú,* p. 25.

MISCELLANEOUS

Killing female animals	Severe punishment [a]
Trespassing without consent [presumably taking or using land of another]	Death [b]
Laziness	Death [b] [c]
Sleeping in the daytime	Beating [d]
Borrowing and not repaying [He who received something entrusted to him must take care of it as his own]	Restitution within one year—if could not pay debt, had to pay in service [e]
Witchcraft to commit a crime	Death [f]
Wearing of silver, gold, precious stones, feathers, garments of vicuna forbidden to commoners	No punishment mentioned [g]
Lying	Punished according to nature of lie [f]
for trivial lies	Hair cut off [f]
Perjury	Beating, 20 blows [h]
Injuring person	Punished and made to maintain one injured; [i] discretionary [j]
Setting fire to house	Damage paid with property and death [k] [l]
Negligent burning of house	Liable for damage [k]
Destroying bridge, malicious intent	Death [j]
Burning bridge	Death [l]
Damaging of field by animal	Owner of field could take value equivalent to damage done from herd [k]
Coca chewing [only allowed commoners with permission of governor]	No penalty mentioned [m]
Drunkenness to point of loss of reason except on particular occasions—these exceptions appear to have been frequent and to have been an occasion for sexual license	Punishable [details not listed here] [n]

[a] Cieza, *Crónica del Perú*, II, 56.
[b] Murúa, *Historia del origen*, III, xx, 211; Cobo, *Historia*, III, xII, xxvi, 241.
[c] "Relación del origen é gobierno," p. 68.
[d] Levillier ed., *Gobernantes del Perú*, IX, 275.
[e] Murúa, *Historia del origen*, III, lxxiii, 353.
[f] De las Casas, *De las antiguas gentes del Perú*, p. 212.
[g] Valera, *Las costumbres antiguas del Perú*, p. 114.
[h] Poma, *Primer nueva corónica*, p. 313.
[i] Levillier ed., *Gobernantes del Perú*, IX, 276.
[j] Levillier ed., *Gobernantes del Perú*, IX, 274.
[k] Levillier ed., *Gobernantes del Perú*, IX, 275.
[l] Cobo, *Historia*, III, xII, xxvi, 240.
[m] Acosta, *Natural and Moral History*, IV, xxii, 246.
[n] Valera, *Las costumbres antiguas del Perú*, pp. 48, 51–52, 56; Ramirez, in Trimborn ed., *Quellen*, p. 61; *Relaciones geográficas*, II, La Paz, p. 72; III, Quito, p. 93; Poma, *Primer nueva corónica*, p. 313; De las Casas, *De las antiguas gentes del Perú*, p. 25.

• GLOSSARY

acllas	young girls of the agriculturalist class permanently taken from their families, first to live in a house of the chosen women in the provincial capital and to be trained in weaving and other skills, and ultimately to be taken to Cuzco to be distributed by the Inca, some for the Sun religion, some to reward those whom the Inca wished to honor, some to serve the Inca's wives. *See* Chap. II.
aine	exchange of labor for labor.
ayllu	Rowe, in *Handbook of South American Indians*, II, 255, defines as "a kin group with theoretical endogamy, with descent in the male line" which "owned a definite territory." It also on occasion means lineage, particularly with reference to the Inca royal *ayllus*. Rowe also indicates its modern usage (*Ibid.*, 253): "a number of unrelated extended families living together in a restricted area and following certain common rules of crop rotation under more or less informal leaders . . . community."
cacique	Arawak word used by the Spanish in Peru for chiefs or officials. Spanish equivalent to Quechua *curaca*.
chosen women	*see* acllas.
cumbi cloth	tapestry cloth with feathers woven into it.
curaca	Quechua word for chief. Here used for officials up to the rank of Inca governor.
guaca	*see* huaca.
guaranga	chief of 1,000.
huaca	sacred place, object, spirit.
hunu	chief of 10,000.
mita	labor service. *See* Chap. II.
orejones	the Inca class, reference to ear deformation which served as a mark of nobility.
pachaca	chief of 100.
tambo	provisioned resting house on the royal roads.
tokoy-rikoq	inspecting official sent by the Inca central government.
t'oqrikoq	provincial governor.
tupu	amount of land allotted out of community lands for each agriculturist and his wife.
yungas	certain northern coastal plains and valleys; *yunga* is the Quechua name for language spoken in the northern half of the Chimu kingdom.

• BIBLIOGRAPHY

Acosta, José de. *Natural and Moral History of the Indies,* edited by C. R. Markham, London, 1880.

Acosta, José de. *Historia natural y moral de last Indias,* 2 vols. Madrid, 1894.

Anavitarte, Carlos Núñez. *El cacicazgo como supervivencia "Esclavista-Patriarcal" en el seno de la sociedad colonial,* Cuzco, 1955.

Avila, Francisco de. "A Narrative of the Errors, False Gods, and other Superstitions which the Indians of Huarochiri lived in Ancient Times," in *The Rites and Laws of the Yncas,* translated by C. R. Markham, London, 1873, pp. 122-47.

Bandera, Damian de la. "Relación general de la disposición y calidad de la provincia de Guamanga (1557)," in *Relaciones geográficas,* edited by Jiménez de la Espada, 4 vols. Vol. 1, Madrid 1881-1897.

Bandera, Damian de la. "Relación de señores indios que sirvieron a Tupac Yupanqui y Huayna Capac (1557)," in *Colección de libros y documentos referentes á la historia del Perú,* edited by H. H. Urteaga and Carlos Romero, III, Series 2, Lima, 1920, pp. 55-57.

Basadre, Jorge. *Historia del derecho peruana,* Lima, 1937.

Baudin, Louis. *L'Empire socialiste des Inka,* Paris, 1928.

Benayas, Juan. *Los mitos comunistas, socialistas y colectivistas del Perú prehispano.* Lima, 1951.

Betanzos, Juan de. "Suma y narración de los incas," *Biblioteca Hispano-Ultramarina,* Vol. V, edited by Marcos Jiménez de la Espada, Madrid, 1880.

Boletín bibliográfico de antropología americana, Instituto panamericano de geografía e historia, Mexico, 1937-1955.

Bonthoux, Adolphe-Victor, *Le Régime Économique des Incas,* Marseille, 1927.

Borregán, Alonso. *Crónica de la conquista del Perú,* edited by Rafael Loredo, Sevilla, 1948.

Bram, Joseph. *An Analysis of Inca Militarism,* New York, 1941.

Cabello de Balboa, Miguel. "Historia del Perú bajo la dominación de los Incas," *Colección de libros y documentos referentes á la historia del Perú*, edited by H. H. Urteaga and C. Romero, Vol. II, Series 2, Lima, 1920.

Cabello Valboa, Miguel. *Miscelánea antártica*, Lima, 1951.

Calancha, Antonio de. "Corónica moralizada," *Los cronistas de convento*, edited by José de la Riva Agüero, Series 1, No. 4, Paris, 1938.

Castro, Cristóbal de, and Ortega Morejón, Diego de. "Relación y declaración del modo que este valle de Chincha y sus comarcanos se gobernaban antes que hobiese ingas y despues que les hobo hasta que los cristianos entraron en esta tierra," *Quellen zur Kulturgeschichte des präkolumbischen Amerika*, edited and translated by Hermann Trimborn, Stuttgart, 1936.

Castro Pozo, Hildebrando. "Social and Economico-Political Evolution of the Communities of Central Peru," *Handbook of South American Indians*, Washington, 1947, II, 483–99.

Cieza de León, Pedro de. *The Travels of Pedro Cieza de León*, edited and translated by Clements R. Markham, London, 1864.

——— *Segunda parte de la crónica del Perú*, edited by Jiménez de la Espada, Biblioteca Hispano-Ultramarina, Vol. II, Madrid, 1880.

Clagett, Helen. *A Guide to the Law of Peru*, Washington, 1947.

Cobo, El Padre Bernabé. *Historia del Nuevo Mundo*, edited by Jiménez de la Espada, Seville, 1892.

Colección de documentos inéditos relativos al descubrimiento conquista y colonización de las posesiones españoles en America y Oceania, sacados en su mayor parte, de Real Archivo de Indias, 42 vols. Madrid, 1864–1884.

Colección de libros y documentos referentes a la historia del Perú, edited by Horacio H. Urteaga and Carlos Romero, I–XII, Series 1, Lima 1916–1919; I–XI, Series 2, Lima, 1920–1939.

Cunow, Heinrich. *Die Soziale Verfassung des Inkareichs*, Stuttgart, 1896.

De las Casas, Bartolomé. *De las antiguas gentes del Perú*, edited by Marcos Jiménez de la Espada, in *Colección de libros españoles raros ó curiosos*, Vol. XXI, Madrid, 1892.

Estete, Miguel de. "La relación de viage que hizo el Señor Hernando Pizaro . . . desde el pueblo de Caxamalca a Pascama y de allí á Xauxa," *El descubrimiento y la conquista del Perú*, edited by Carlos M. Larrea, 3, Quito, 1918, 300–50.

——— "Noticia del Perú," *Los cronistas de la conquista*, Biblioteca de cultura peruana, edited by Horacio H. Urteaga, Series 1, No. 2, Paris, 1938.

Falcón, Francisco. "Relación sobre el gobierno de los Incas," *Colección de libros y documentos referentes a la historia del Perú*, XI, Series 1, Lima, 1918, 135–76.

Garcilaso de la Vega. *The Royal Commentaries of the Yncas*, edited by Clements R. Markham, 2 vols. London, 1869.

Gibson, Charles. "The Inca Concept of Sovereignty and the Spanish Administration in Peru," in *University of Texas Latin-American Studies*, IV, Austin, 1948.

Gobernantes del Perú, cartas y papeles siglo XVI, 14 vols. Documentos del Archivo de Indias, Colección de publicaciones históricas de la biblioteca del congreso argentino, edited by D. Roberto Levillier, Madrid, 1925.

"El gobierno del Inga era por el orden siguiente," in *Colección de libros y documentos referentes á la historia del Perú*, edited by H. H. Urteaga, III, Series 2, Lima, 1920, 77–86.

González Holguín, Diego. *Vocabulario de la lengua general de todo el Perú llamada lengua Qquichua*, Lima, 1608.

Handbook of Latin American Studies, Cambridge, Massachusetts, 1935–1957.

Handbook of South American Indians, edited by Julian H. Steward, Vols. II and V, Washington, D.C., 1947, 1949.

Hoebel, E. Adamson. *The Law of Primitive Man*, Cambridge, 1954.

"Horden que el Ynga tubo en la governación del Piru," (unpublished manuscript, British Museum, Add. MS. 13, 992, Fol. 411–15). Material in many parts is identical with "Relación del origen é gobierno . . ."

Jiménez de la Espada, Marcos, editor, *Relaciones geográficas de Indias*, 4 vols. Madrid, 1881–1897.

——— *Tres relaciones de antigüedades peruanas*, Madrid, 1879.

Latcham, Ricardo A. "El dominio de la tierra y el sistema tributario en el antiguo imperio de los Incas," in *Revista chilena de historia y geografía*, LII (1927), 201–57.

Le Riverend, Dr. Julio. *Crónicas de la conquista del Perú*, Mexico.

Levillier, Roberto, editor, *Gobernantes del Perú, cartas y papeles siglo XVI*, 14 vols. Madrid, 1921–1926.

——— *Don Francisco de Toledo, supremo organizador del Perú, su vida, su obra*, Vol. II, Buenos Aires, 1940.

Lizarraga, Fray Reginaldo de. "Descripción breve de toda la tierra del Perú," *Los cronistas de convento*, Series I, No. 4, edited by José de la Riva Agüero, Paris, 1938.

Markham, Clements R. *Narratives of the Rites and Laws of the Yncas*, London, 1873.

Marof, Tristan. *La Justicia del Inca,* Brussels, 1926.

Matienzo, Juan de. *Gobierno del Perú,* Buenos Aires, 1910.

McCown, Theodore Doney. *Pre-Incaic Huamachuco,* Berkeley, 1945.

Means, Philip Ainsworth. *Ancient Civilizations of the Andes,* New York, 1936.

—— "Biblioteca Andina," in *Transactions of the Connecticut Academy of Arts and Sciences,* XXIX (1928), 271–525.

—— "A Study of Ancient Andean Social Institutions," in *Transactions of the Connecticut Academy of Arts and Sciences,* XXVII, (1925) 407–69.

Molina, Cristóbal (de Cuzco), and Cristóbal (de Santiago) Molina. *Las crónicas de los Molinas,* Los pequeños grandes libros de historia americana, Vol. IV, Series 1, Lima, 1943.

Montesinos, Fernando de. *Memorias antiguas historiales y políticas del Perú,* Colección de libros y documentos referentes á la historia del Perú, edited by H. H. Urteaga and C. Romero, Vol. XVI, Series 2, Lima, 1930.

Morúa, Martín de. *Historia del origen y genealogía de los reyes Incas del Perú,* Colección de libros y documentos referentes á la historia del Perú, edited by H. H. Urteaga and C. Romero, Vol. IV, Series 2, Lima, 1922.

Murdock, George Peter. *Our Primitive Contemporaries,* Macmillan, New York, 1934.

Murra, John V. "The Economic Organization of the Inca State," (unpublished Ph.D dissertation, University of Chicago, 1956).

Murúa, Martín de. *Historia del orígen y genealogía real de los reyes Incas del Perú,* edited by Constantino Bayle, S.J., Madrid, 1946.

Pizarro, Hernando. "A los magníficos señores, los señores oidores de la Audiencia real de S.M. que reside en la ciudad de Sto-Domingo," in *Los cronistas de la conquista,* edited by H. H. Urteaga, Biblioteca de cultura peruana, Series 1, No. 2, Paris, 1938.

Pizarro, Pedro. *Relation of the Discovery and Conquest of the Kingdoms of Peru,* edited and translated by P. A. Means, 2 vols. New York, 1921.

Polo de Ondegardo, Juan. "Relación de los fundamentos acerca del notable daño que resulta de no guardar á los indios sus fueros." "De la orden que los Yndios tenyan en dividir los tributos e destribuyr los entre si," in *Colección de documentos inéditos del Archivo de Indias,* XVII, Madrid, 1864–1884, 5–177.

——— "Report," *The Rites and Laws of the Yncas*, edited and translated by Clements R. Markham, London, 1873.

——— Informaciones acerca de la religión y gobierno de los Incas. *Colección de libros y documentos referentes á la historia del Perú*, Vols. III, IV, Series 1, Lima, 1916, 1917.

Poma de Ayala, Phelipe Guaman. *Primer nueva corónica y buen gobierno*, edited by A. Posnansky, La Paz, Bolivia, 1944.

Prescott, William H. *History of the Conquest of Mexico and History of the Conquest of Peru*, New York, 1936.

"Relación de las costumbres antiguas de los naturales del Pirú," *Tres relaciones de antigüedades Peruanas*, edited by Jiménez de la Espada, Madrid, 1879, pp. 137–227. (Apparently written by Valera, though published here as anonymous.)

"Relación del origen é gobierno que los Ingas tuvieron . . . ," in *Colección de libros y documentos referentes á la historia del Perú*, Vol. III, Series 2, Lima, 1920, 55–77. (Apparently written by Damian de la Bandera.)

Relaciones geográficas de Indias, edited by Marcos Jiménez de la Espada, 4 vols., Madrid, 1881–1897.

Riva Agüero, José de la. *Los cronistas de convento*. Series 1, No. 4, Paris, 1938.

Rodríguez del Busto, N. "Organización y aplicación de la justicia en el tiempo incaico," Conferencia ante la Junta de Historia, y Numismática, Tucuman (?), 1925.

Roman y Zamora, Jerónimo. *Repúblicas de Indias idolatrías y gobierno en México y Perú antes de la conquista*, in *Colección de libros raros o curiosos que tratan de America*, Vols. XIV, XV, Madrid, 1897.

Rowe, John Howland. "Inca Culture at the Time of the Spanish Conquest," in *Handbook of South American Indians*, edited by Julian Steward, II, Washington, 1947, 183–330.

——— "The Kingdom of Chimor," *Acta Americana*, Vol. VI, Mexico, 1948.

Sancho de la Hoz, Pedro. "Relación para S.M. de lo sucedido en la conquista y pacificación de estas provincias de la nueva Castilla," in *Los cronistas de la conquista*, edited by H. H. Urteaga, Biblioteca de cultura peruana, Series 1, No. 2, Paris, 1938.

Santillán, Fernando de. "Relación del origen, descendencia, política y gobierno de los Incas," *Tres relaciones*, edited by Jiménez de la Espada, Madrid, 1879.

Sarmiento de Gamboa, Pedro. *Historia de los Incas*, 2d ed., Buenos Aires, 1942.

Toledo, Don Francisco de. See Levillier.

Trimborn, Hermann. "Straftat und Sühne in Alt-Peru," *Zeitschrift für Ethnologie*, LVII, Berlin, 1925, 194–240.

—— *Quellen zur Kulturgeschichte des präkolumbischen Amerika*, Stuttgart, 1936.

——"Der Kollectivismus der Inkas in Peru," *Anthropos*, XVIII–XIX, Vienna, 1923, 1924, 978–1001; XX, Vienna, 1925, 579–606.

—— "Familien und Erbrecht im präkolumbischen Peru," in *Zeitschrift für Vergleichende Rechtswissenschaft*, XLII, Stuttgart, 1927, 352–92.

—— "Die Methode der ethnologischen Rechtsforschung," in *Zeitschrift für Vergleichende Rechtswissenschaft*, XLIII, Stuttgart, 1928, 416–64.

—— "Der Rechtsbruch in den Hochkulturen Amerikas," *Zeitschrift für vergleichende Rechtswissenschaft*, LI, Stuttgart, 1937, 8–129.

—— "Der Magische und religiöse Gehalt des altperianischen Rechts," in *Zeitschrift für vergleichende Rechtswissenschaft*, LVIII, Stuttgart (1955), 41–47.

—— "Die Organisation der öffentlichen Gewalt im Inka-Reich," in *Festschrift Publication d'Hommage offerte à P.W. Schmidt*, Vienna, 1928, pp. 740–59.

Steward, Julian. "South American Cultures: An Interpretive Summary," *Handbook of South American Indians*, Washington, 1949, 669–72.

Urteaga, Horacio H., editor, *Los cronistas de la conquista*, Biblioteca de cultura peruana, Series 1, No. 2, Paris, 1938.

—— "La organización judicial en el imperio de los Incas," *Revista histórica de Lima*, Series 9, 1928.

Urteaga, Horacio H. and Carlos Romero, editors. *Colección de libros y documentos referentes á la historia del Perú*, Vols. I–XII, Series 1, Lima, 1916–1919; Vols. I–XI, Series 2, Lima, 1920–1939.

Valcárcel, Luís E. "Indian Markets and Fairs in Peru," *Handbook of South American Indians*, II, Washington, D.C., 1947, 477–82.

—— *Historia de la cultura antigua del Perú*, 2 vols. Vol. 1, Lima, 1943, Vol. II, Lima, 1948.

Valdes de la Torre, Carlos. "Régimen de la propriedad durante los Incas," in *Mercurio Peruana*, V, Lima, 1920, 399–413.

Valera, Blas. *Las costumbres antiguas del Perú y la historia de los Incas*, Los pequeños grandes libros de historia Americana, Vol. VIII, Series 1, Lima, 1945.

Vargas Ugarte, Rubén. *Historia del Perú, Fuentes,* Lima, 1939.

Xerez, Francisco de. "Verdadera relación de la conquista del Perú," in *Crónicas de las conquista del Perú,* edited by Dr. Julio le Riverend, Colección Atenea, Mexico, 194–.

Zurkalowski, Erich. "Observaciones sobre la organización social de Perú antiguo," in *Mercurio Peruana,* II, No. 11, (1919) 337 ff.; No. 12, 480 ff.

• INDEX

Accountants (*quipucamayos*), 114
Acllas, 81, 175; *see also* "House of the Chosen Women"
Acosta, José de, cited, 25, 36, 46, 75, 93, 95
Adultery, 78-79, 170
Aged, sick and the, 21, 59-60, 62, 81
Agricultural lands, 21-38; *see also* Community lands; Inca lands; Sun lands
Agriculture, 2, 3; *see also* specific subjects, e.g., Produce
Aine system, 58, 175
Apocunas (royal council), 94, 99, 111, 123
Apopanaca, 67
Aristocracy, 15; *see also* Nobility
Army service, 12, 21, 59, 62, 110, 115
Ashanti kingdom, 122-23
Ayllus (communities), 22, 23, 159, 174; legal functions of, 42, 80; title and usufruct as between the Inca and, 46-47; tax system, 50 (*see also* Tax system); land system, 97 (*see also* Community lands)
Ayllus, royal, 100, 111-12, 117, 123
Aztec Mexico: land system in, 19; lawbreaking and penalties in, 76, 83-84, 133; commercial development in, 89, 132; laws of inheritance in, 91; government in, 123

Bandera, Damian de la, cited, 30, 46, 59, 95, 97
Barter, use of, 86-89, 132
Baudin, Louis, cited, 5, 7, 17, 46, 75, 129
Benedict, Ruth, 127
Borregán, Alonso, cited, 86
Boundary markers, 43, 46, 166
Bram, Joseph, cited, 11, 26
Bridges, building and maintainance of, 51, 61; penalties for harming, 174
Building: labor draft for, 48, 51-52, 62, 110; taxation for, 58, 68

Building materials, 38
Buildings, 3, 41; *see also* specific types, e.g., Palaces
Bureaucracy, Inca, 12-15, 58, 72, 90, 98, 131, 133

Cabello de Balboa, Miguel, cited, 34, 84, 94
Cacique, defined, 28, 174; land ownership by, 28, 36, 42, 53-54; and mining, 39-40, 55-56, 57; household service for, 51; gifts to the Inca presented by, 54-55; and craft production, 54-58; inheritance of the position of, 90; succession of, 94-95, 96; punishment of, 116, 167; *see also* Curaca; Governing officials
Cajas, 40
Capaocha, 81, 119
Casas, Bartolomé de las: *see* Las Casas
Castro, Cristóbal de, and Ortega Morejón, Diego de, cited, 8, 26, 30, 35, 37, 59, 94, 95, 97-98
Census system, 12, 128, 132; taxation and, 66, 101, 109, 115, 116, 124; use of *quipos* in, 119
Chasquis, 115
Chibcha, lawbreaking among, 83-84
Chimu (or Chimor) kingdom, influence on Inca empire after conquest, 14-15, 18, 20-21, 28-29, 30, 53, 100, 121, 141
Chincha Valley: land rights in, 26, 28, 29-30, 35, 36, 37, 59, 65, 94-95, 97-98; water rights in, 39
Chosen women, *see* House of the Chosen Women
Chunca, 99
Cieza de León, Pedro de, cited, 7, 31, 33, 34, 51, 57, 65, 67, 68, 86, 95, 96
Class structure, 2, 5-6, 22, 93; *see also* specific classes, e.g., Nobility, Cacique, Curaca, Inca

Date Due